W9-BSG-777

MARILYN MONROE

The Pictorial Treasury of Film Stars

MARILYN MONROE

by

Joan Mellen

General Editor: **TED SENNETT**

GALAHAD BOOKS • NEW YORK CITY

This Galahad Books edition is published by
arrangement with Pyramid Communications, Inc.

ISBN 0-88365-165-3

Library of Congress Catalog Card Number 73-90218

Printed in the United States of America

FOR RALPH
ONE OF THE FEW MEN WHO WOULD HAVE RESPECTED
MARILYN MONROE

PREFACE

By Ted Sennett

"The movies!" Flickering lights in the darkness that stirred our imaginations and haunted our dreams. All of us cherish memories of "going to the movies" to gasp at feats of derring-do, to roar with laughter at clownish antics, to weep at acts of noble sacrifice. For many filmgoers, the events on the screen were not only larger than life but also more mysterious, more fascinating, and—when times were bad—more rewarding. And if audiences could be blamed for preferring movies to life, they never seemed to notice, or care.

Of course the movies have always been more than a source of wish-fulfillment or a repository for nostalgic memories. From the first unsteady images to today's most experimental efforts, motion pictures have mirrored America's social history, and over the decades they have developed into an internationally esteemed art.

As social history, movies reflect our changing tastes, styles, and ideas. To our amusement, they show us how we looked and behaved: flappers with bobbed hair and bee-stung lips cavorting at "wild" parties; gangsters and G-men in striped suits and wide-brimmed hats exchanging gunfire in city streets; pompadoured "swing-shift" Susies and dashing servicemen, "working for Uncle Sam." To our chagrin, they show us the innocent (and sometimes not so innocent) lies we believed: that love triumphs over all adversity and even comes to broad-shouldered lady executives; that war is an heroic and virtually bloodless activity; that fame and success can be achieved indiscriminately by chorus girls, scientists, football players, and artists. To our edification, they show us how we felt about marriage in the twenties, crime in the thirties, war in the forties, big business in the fifties, and youth in the sixties. (Presumably future filmgoers will know how we felt about sex in the seventies.)

As an influential art, motion pictures are being studied and analyzed as never before by young filmgoers who are excited by the medium's past accomplishments and its even greater potential for the future. The rich body of films from *Intolerance* to *The Godfather;* the work of directors from Griffith to Kubrick; the uses of film for documenting events, ideas, and even emotions—these are the abundant materials from which film courses and film societies are being created across the country.

THE PICTORIAL TREASURY OF FILM STARS also draws on these materials, encompassing in a series of publications all the people, the trends, and the concepts that have contributed to motion pictures as nostalgia, as social history, and as art. The books in the series range as widely as the camera-eye can take us, from the distant past when artists with a vision of film's possibilities shaped a new form of expression, to the immediate future, when the medium may well undergo changes as innovative as the first primitive movements.

THE PICTORIAL TREASURY OF FILM STARS is a tribute to achievement: to the charismatic stars who linger in all our memories, and to the gifted people behind the cameras: the directors, the producers, the writers, the editors, the cameramen. It is also a salute to everyone who loves movies, forgives their failures, and acknowledges their shortcomings, who attends Bogart and Marx Brothers revivals and Ingmar Bergman retrospectives and festivals of forthcoming American and European films.

"The movies!" The cameras turn and the flickering images begin. And again we settle back to watch the screen, hoping to see a dream made real, an idea made palpable, or a promise fulfilled. On that unquenchable hope alone, the movies will endure.

ACKNOWLEDGMENTS

I wish to express my appreciation to the following people for their help and kindness: Linda Cutler, for generously giving of her time in painstaking research; Rita Morucci, Film Librarian at Temple University, for her assistance and for making available to me the facilities of Temple in viewing the films of Marilyn Monroe; Martin Bresnick of Audio-Brandon Films, distributors of *How To Marry A Millionaire,* for extraordinary generosity and cooperation, providing films gratis and performing an invaluable service to critics and historians of film; my friend Adeline Weiner, who discussed Marilyn Monroe with me and provided many helpful insights; Michael Hamilburg, for the rare friendship and encouragement for all my writing that comes but seldom in a person's lifetime; and most of all, my husband, Ralph Schoenman, who painstakingly read the manuscript, suggesting many ideas and interpretations as well as providing his usual moral support. For the photographs, the editor would like to thank Jerry Vermilye and *Movie Star News.*

CONTENTS

MARILYN MONROE

CHAPTER I

THE MONROE IMAGE

Ten years after her death, the woman Marilyn Monroe continues to haunt us. Her films and her life became interchangeable because Hollywood producers would have her believe that she was playing herself in the host of films which treated her as America's favorite sex symbol. At the end of *The Seven Year Itch*, Tom Ewell accounts to a friend for the blonde in his kitchen, saying "maybe it's Marilyn Monroe." She is given no name in this film other than "The Girl" because she exists only as the living fantasy of a neurotic middle-aged husband beset by a wife in the country and a persistent "itch" for sensuality.

None of her films could be considered examples of film art. All were packaged according to a Hollywood formula begun after the Second World War and pursued by Twentieth Century-Fox with a vengeance through its pin-up queen, Betty Grable. Marilyn inherited her mantle, as well as dressing room "M" at Fox. Her films sold "love" and sex as the sole means by which a woman could find fulfillment.

Yet the image of Marilyn Monroe continues to appeal to us because she represented more than the sex symbol whose ample breasts guaranteed her money and fame. The deprivations of Marilyn Monroe's childhood have by now become legendary. She was born an illegitimate child of a woman who would spend the majority of her life institutionalized and whose own mother died in an insane asylum. In fact, Marilyn's mother stabbed her best friend, Grace McKee, with a kitchen knife shortly after Marilyn's birth. One of Monroe's earliest and most disturbing memories was that of her grandmother pressing a pillow down on her face shortly before the deranged woman was finally committed to a state hospital. Marilyn's mother, Gladys Baker—like her mother, father, and brother—was diagnosed a "paranoid schizophrenic."

During a long childhood featuring a succession of foster homes in most of which she was made to feel unwanted and scorned, Marilyn Monroe would call Clark Gable her "secret father." Hollywood had provided her with a fantasy father as a child even as she herself would be made into an embodied sexual fantasy. It was almost out of a Hollywood script that in her last film she would play opposite the very Gable she had dreamed of as a deprived child. The final drive into the darkness at the end of *The Mis-*

590

THE SEVEN YEAR ITCH (1955).
With Tom Ewell

fits must have been particularly significant to her. It captured one modality of what Marilyn Monroe had sought all her life: the father who would protect and accept her. Endlessly she attempted to create situations approximating this early need as she re-enacted the traumas of her childhood. Through alcohol and drugs she sought desperately to suppress the terror that she would always be alone, unvalued and unloved.

Unprotected, the little girl Marilyn became vulnerable to hurt and abuse which recurrently haunted her as an adult. In her early adolescence, while she was living with her guardian Grace McKee, McKee's husband Doc Goddard embraced and kissed the girl too intimately. Marilyn, or Norma Jean as she was then, was forced to move in with Grace's maiden aunt, Ana Lower. "I always felt insecure," Marilyn Monroe later understated. Shunted from family to family, she was sometimes forced to abide by the sternest codes of a simultaneously puritanical and prurient culture, including, with one family, three separate church sessions each Sunday.

A few guardians were lax and easy, like the English couple with whom she lived for a time and who allowed her to spend Saturdays at the movies. There she clung to a fantasy world, anticipating the woman who would later shun anything which reminded her of Norma Jean in her need to become what she was cruelly induced to believe was the "free" woman projected on Hollywood screens. Hers was a childhood in which she was made to feel ashamed of her very existence. As if an outcast, she bore a stigma of which she was constantly reminded. One of her cruel foster mothers even said to her, "Stop calling me mama. I'm not your mama. I'm not related to you at all. You just board here."

It is not difficult to see how a child made to feel undeserving of love became the woman who would make herself at once desirable, self-effacing and vulnerable so that men could not help but admire her. As an adult, Marilyn Monroe would be accused of embellishing the abuses of her childhood and charged even with fabricating details. An example involved her treatment in a Los Angeles orphanage. The head mistress swore that the children were not in fact made to wash endless amounts of dishes for a nickel a day, as Marilyn Monroe had claimed.

The point must remain moot. Whether or not she was beaten with a hairbrush or forced to bathe in filthy water, the common denominator of all these years was the trauma of feeling totally unworthy of respect, appreciation or love.

Early publicity pose

To this must be added rape at the age of nine, an onslaught producing a stammer which never completely left her. The whispery, baby voice associated with Marilyn Monroe conveyed transparently her appeal for protection and her desire for a childhood purged of the brutality of being unwanted and ill-used. Her demeanor was a plea to be sheltered as children have a right to be, shielded from outrages like the rape, which has been well documented. The star boarder of one of Marilyn's foster mothers lured her into his room and violated her. When she hesitantly reported the event, her foster mother slapped the child across the face for daring to "accuse such a good man of something so terrible." When Norma Jean was given a coin for "cooperating," she flung it down the stairs. It is doubtful she ever erased the memory.

There is a slim volume called *Violations Of The Child Marilyn Monroe** purportedly written by a psychiatrist-lover of Monroe's near the end of her life. He describes a series of child molestations suffered by her and confessed to him by Marilyn. These began with a group molestation by a gang of boys barely older than the tomboy Norma Jean and include a sequel to the rape by a "garbage man" as well as by the father of a childhood friend.

*Bridgehead Books: New York, 1962.

Published anonymously by a company with an unlisted street address and telephone number, the book has the flavor of a further exploitation of Marilyn Monroe disguised as a sympathetic account of a grisly childhood. Yet although James Dougherty, Marilyn's first husband, has insisted that she was a virgin when they married, the evidence and Marilyn's own testimony make clear that, at a minimum, the incident in the boarding house did occur. Like the name of her prominent last lover, there are corners of the life of Marilyn Monroe which will probably remain obscure.

Throughout her life, Marilyn Monroe remained unsure of the identity of her father, although she finally accepted a man named C. Stanley Gifford who worked alongside Gladys Baker at Consolidated Film Industries where Baker assembled negatives. In 1950, quite early in her career, Monroe made an attempt to see Gifford. Phoning ahead, she was told that if she had any complaints, she should speak to his lawyer in Los Angeles, a comment Marilyn repeated later in her life when Gifford tried to see *her*.

Baffled by insecurity, Marilyn Monroe struggled for some means of transcending the role of victim. As for so many American children of her generation, films repre-

sented an alternative world, free of the grime and tawdriness of the day-to-day. The Hollywood of her time displayed women of consummate physical perfection who attracted men overcome by gratitude and willing to declare eternal devotion. Such films molded the expectations of girls like Norma Jean, leading them to wish for fathers like Clark Gable or strong, silent husbands like Joe DiMaggio. As these films helped them escape from the drab boredom of their own lives, they simultaneously diminished the real world incalculably. They presented scenarios of inevitable and permanently happy marriage, free either of social or personal conflict in which even old age rarely intruded. Through this mythical world in which reality was sacrificed to a facade of saccharine sentiment, Norma Jean Baker fled the emotional deprivations of her youth.

Marilyn Monroe attempted to escape exploitation by becoming a "star," and affecting a vapid, little-girl quality designed to appeal to men. The Joan Crawfords and Katharine Hepburns in their shoulderpads and man-tailored shirts could charm only the most eccentric of men—and then only when they attempted to hide their boldness behind frills and tears. The dumb if innocent blonde with the whispery voice that was "Marilyn Monroe" freed Norma Jean, but, paradoxically, became at the same time a means of enslaving others to an impoverished and demeaning conception of what it meant to be a woman. And Marilyn herself became the prime victim of this image.

Although she aspired to be taken seriously as an actress, she could never quite escape the tinsel persona of sex queen, created for her and first sought by Monroe herself as a way out of deprivation. In her last interview she pleaded with the journalist not "to make (her) a joke," yet not even as president of her own film company could she find a role in which her proffered body did not determine her character and her fate. Monroe herself selected Terence Rattigan's *The Sleeping Prince* as the first vehicle of her liberation and entree as a serious actress, only to play the guileless showgirl Elsie Marina, whose undulating walk ending the film merely parodies the caricatured strut made famous by Marilyn Monroe from *Niagara* on.

The antecedent for the Monroe image in Hollywood is that of Mae West, but West used her sexuality as a means to liberation. She deployed the very physical attributes through which women had been victimized to free herself from the assumed role of passive, simpering recipient of the favors

and guidance of men. Both women were blonde and buxom; both were willing to display themselves to the camera. If Mae West wore costumes remarkably daring for the 1930s, Marilyn Monroe, twenty years later, went further, posing nude for a calendar and baring herself in several films. These included *The Misfits,* whose nude scene delighted all but director John Huston, who cut it, and *Bus Stop,* where Marilyn so distracted Don Murray that he read "pale and scaly" for "pale and white" in their bedroom scene. (With some hostility Marilyn congratulated him on his Freudian slip!)

Mae West had used her famous one-liners to achieve independence and autonomy ("I'm the regal type—that is not a posture you learn in school, dearie. It's the way you look at the world"), and Monroe occasionally tried to emulate her. Asked what she had on when she posed for the famous nude calendar, she replied, "the radio!" When she was accused of wearing falsies, she retorted, "Those who know me better, know better." In 1952 she spoke about "the things a gal has to think up to outwit predatory males." Mae West never attempted to achieve her freedom except as a sex symbol, but in her films she emerges as a many-sided, imaginative woman who could take over a schoolroom of unruly boys on occasion or argue her own case in a breach-of-promise trial. West's lasciviousness gave her room to create a persona capable of generosity and free choice.

Marilyn Monroe shared the role of sex symbol, but, unlike West's, it was a persona, not of autonomy, but of exaggerated subservience and incapacity. For Monroe's image was that favored both in Hollywood and in the culture in general—an empty-headed wide-eyed dumb blonde enticing men but rarely earning their respect for her talent or character. Monroe, like West, was adored by homosexuals because of her powerful suggestion of the female impersonator through an exaggerated walk heightened by sheathlike dresses several sizes too small.

Where Mae West transcends the role—uses it cynically and invests it with irony and parody—Monroe is reduced by it to a persona of giddy innocence and simple-minded vulnerability. She is utterly without guile, as if to be childlike cancels out the real meaning of exposing her breasts on the screen to salivating if contemptuous men.

Where West manipulated and ridiculed, Monroe appears more pathetic than ever, an injured waif. Unlike West, it is she who is rendered ridiculous unawares, still the creature pleading for understanding, but allowing herself to recede into the role with which she began as a model and fastened upon herself from *The Asphalt Jungle* and *All About Eve* to *Let's Make Love* and *The Misfits*.

Mae West, with the exception of one adolescent interlude, remained unmarried all her life. Marilyn Monroe, in all respects the little Norma Jean sent to the movies every Saturday afternoon, wished from each of her three marriages for the obliteration of self expected of American women and celebrated in the films on which they had been nurtured. "Joe doesn't have to move a muscle," she said while married to DiMaggio. "Treat a husband this way and he'll enjoy you twice as much."

CHAPTER II.

MIND AND BODY

"I've been tryin' to be somebody."
Marilyn Monroe as Cherie in BUS STOP.

From a plain if sweet-looking teenager who had been called at one point "the mouse" and at another "the human bean," Norma Jean transformed herself into Marilyn Monroe, accentuating through make-up and dress the physical attributes of an otherwise ordinary girl. In high school she began to wear tight sweaters and very heavy make-up, inspiring taunting responses from her peers, to whom Norma Jean would reply, "Why not? It's my face."

As soon as she began modeling for Emmeline Snively in Hollywood, she was encouraged to dye her hair a true blonde. She exercised with weights at least forty minutes each day. In 1948, under the tutelage of Freddie Karger of Columbia Pictures, she managed to arrange orthodontia on credit for her protruding front teeth, and she diligently wore her detachable retainer many hours a day to correct the imperfection. When Johnny Hyde became her agent in 1950, he saw to it that a small lump was removed from the tip of her nose through plastic surgery. Her chin line was strengthened during the same operation by the addition of cartilage to her jaw.

The image of exaggerated sexuality projected by Monroe was thus entirely a creation of herself and of her Hollywood advisors packaging a product and putting together a sex symbol with surgical knife, bandages, and bodily distortion. Monroe did not protest, although part of the legend is that she had not wanted to dye and straighten her hair, but was faced with the threat that she would lose a well-paying modeling job. Obsessed by ambition and the need to be a star, Marilyn did what she was told and became the stereotype promoted in all her films. The new "Marilyn Monroe" learned to smile so that her nose would not seem too long. She had an excessively high gum line and through great practice learned to "lower her smile," so that the gums would not show. The famous Monroe smile with parted lips rigidly in place, wet and dripping carmine red, was as much to conceal the flaw as to announce sexual readiness.

What helped to make a success of the package was that such flaws were transformed into virtues. They were made part of the unique apparatus of the symbol and a trademark not easily imitated by others. Although in its pique over Monroe's uncooperativeness

GENTLEMEN PREFER BLONDES (1953). As Loreli

SOMETHING'S GOT TO GIVE
(1962, uncompleted)

Twentieth Century-Fox tried to replace her with such starlets as Sheree North, the public relations on Monroe was too far advanced and she survived.

By the end of her career Marilyn Monroe was tired of the symbol which left so little space for her true self to surface. In a few shots extant from the costume tests of the unfinished *Something's Got To Give* Marilyn smiles into the camera and, almost diabolically, for one of the few times in her career, permits her high gum line to show. Unmindful of maintaining the façade, when it was already too late, she tried to emerge as herself.

Her decision to discard the net flesh-colored swimsuit and perform in the nude in this last film has similar roots. It is Marilyn Monroe shedding the false self which once liberated her from poverty, obscurity, and an unfulfilled fantasy life and which she had to destroy to find some measure of worth. By then it was too late. The myth had devoured the woman. The person Norma Jean was so long abandoned by the exigencies of being "Marilyn" that the fear of allowing "the mouse" to emerge drove Marilyn Monroe deeper into pills and alcohol. At the same time, she felt pride in the body that had at least created a Marilyn Monroe behind whom the shy, frightened Norma Jean could hide.

There was another side to "Marilyn Monroe," one disdained and ridiculed by the press, but emergent throughout her life nevertheless. Norma Jean Baker had left high school after the tenth grade to marry Jim Dougherty at the age of sixteen. Throughout her life she sought to make up for the cultural deprivations of her childhood. Although the press would scorn the "unread books" she carried around with her, from her earliest days in Hollywood as a contract player Marilyn Monroe read vociferously, opening charge accounts at bookstores wherever she lived.

LOVE HAPPY (1950). On the set with Groucho Marx

The more she was transformed into a sex symbol, the more she struggled against submergence into the commodity whose packaging she simultaneously allowed. This was the Marilyn who used Vesalius' drawings on anatomy to practice photographic poses. Although she would soon lose her option at Columbia Pictures, she rejected the advances of Harry Cohn, the head of the studio and one of the movie moguls who was the inspiration for Norman Mailer's Herman Teppis in *The Deer Park.* If in her films she appealed to men only through her body and an innocent charm, in life Marilyn Monroe took pride in refusing to sleep with producers and heads of studios who could have made her struggle for parts so much easier. She was soon dismissed by Columbia, despite her competent work in *Ladies of the Chorus.* Marilyn left Cohn to spend the evening reading Thomas Wolfe's *Look Homeward, Angel.*

A short time later her car was about to be repossessed for missed payments, and for fifty dollars she posed nude for a calendar. She got a one-line part in the Marx Brothers' last film, *Love Happy,* playing a girl who catches the eye of Groucho. Marilyn was sent on a publicity tour for this film. She was asked to read a studio tome on the picture, but instead took with her Freud's *Psychopathology of Everyday Life*, Wolfe's *The Web and The Rock*, Proust's *Swann's Way* and *An Actor Prepares* by Konstantin Stanislavsky. She never read the manuscript entrusted to her by the studio.

Monroe's involvement with Freud and his explanation of neurosis continued for the rest of her life through many years of psychoanalysis. She attempted to put the techniques of Stanislavsky into practice with at least partial success in *Bus Stop* and *The Misfits*. Wolfe appealed to her because he understood so well how the traumas of childhood continue to define and haunt the individual long after he believes he has created a separate identity.

In 1951 Marilyn announced with some pride that her favorite authors were Arthur Miller (whom she had met the preceding year), Tolstoy, Wolfe, and Antoine de Saint-Exupery. At UCLA she took evening courses in art and literature. She studied at the Actors' Lab of Morris Carnovsky, Roman Bohnen and J. Edward Bromberg, always arriving on time for her lessons and sitting in the back row. Rarely did she speak in class.

Her mind lacked training and confidence. But she was a woman forever attempting to grow and to sever in subtle if incomplete ways the Faustian bond she had made with Hollywood. In the form of barbituates, Mephistopheles came to claim her in the end precisely because she could not suppress her deepest feelings, including fear, anxiety, and overwhelming early pain. The barbiturates, like her career, could stay this pain, but only at the cost of obliterating the self. Marilyn Monroe the woman could not have been the dizzy blonde, "the girl" without a name she played in so many films, the persona epitomized by Pola in *How To Marry A Millionaire* who tells David Wayne in all seriousness that "Men aren't attentive to girls who wear glasses." The same woman had traveled anonymously to New York to study the stage version of her previous picture, *Gentlemen Prefer Blondes*.

As time passed, Marilyn Monroe struggled for a seriousness of purpose in her life. She longed to repudiate the symbol and to emerge as a thinking person. Her reading included Joyce's *Ulysses*, *Greek Mythology* by Edith Hamilton, Emerson's *Essays*, Sandburg's *Abraham Lincoln* (recommended by Arthur Miller when they first met), the correspondence of Shaw and Mrs. Patrick Campbell, *Gertrude Lawrence As Mrs. A.*, Keats,

ALL ABOUT EVE (1950). With Bette Davis and George Sanders

Dostoevsky, and Salinger. She said that her favorite poem by Keats was "Ode To A Nightingale," and she kept a copy of the poems of Whitman beside her bed. Before her marriage to DiMaggio, she asked George Cukor to direct her in Zola's *Nana.* He refused, foreshadowing the fate of most of her movie aspirations, including that of playing Grushenka in Dostoevsky's *The Brothers Karamazov.*

No incident better reveals Hollywood's refusal to take Marilyn Monroe seriously than her encounter with Joseph L. Mankiewicz on the set of *All About Eve* in 1949. Marilyn was carrying a copy of the poems of Rainier Maria Rilke. Mankiewicz, bemused, believed he had the right to question the sincerity of her choice of reading matter:

> I asked Marilyn if she knew who he was. She shook her head. "No—Who is he?" I told her that Rilke had been a German poet, that he was dead... and asked her how the hell she came to be reading him at all, much less that particular work of his. Had somebody recommended it to her?*

*"*All About Eve's* Women," *New York* magazine, October 16, 1972, p. 41.

The implications are obvious; the dumb blonde of his film, "Miss Caswell... a graduate of the Copacabana School of Dramatic Arts," could not, by herself, have selected Rilke, let alone know whom he was. The gratuitous cruelty in Mankiewicz's response to the young Marilyn was borne out recently when he told Dick Cavett it was just as well that Monroe died when she did as she couldn't have handled being an aging sex symbol and would undoubtedly, at forty-seven, be alcoholic and pathetic. Mankiewicz, like most of Marilyn's Hollywood associates, attempted to make a self-fulfilling prophecy out of their contemptuous attitude toward the mindless blonde who liked to read. The reply Marilyn made to Mankiewicz is poignant:

> You see, in my whole life I haven't read hardly anything at all. I don't know how to catch up. I don't know where to begin. So what I do is, every now and then I go into the Pickwick [a large Hollywood bookshop] and just look around. I leaf through some books, and when I read something that interests me—I buy the book. Is that wrong?†

More than anything, Monroe's reply reveals that in her desire to be taken seriously she denied the very qualities which would have made it possible. "I don't know how to catch up, I don't know where to begin" indicates a deference to men like Mankiewicz, which encouraged them to discount her as a thinking person. It led them to cast her in one role after another as the sensuous, innocent blonde devoid of logic, coherence, and rationality. It enabled them to produce an image which would lead men and women to dissociate beauty from intelligence in women. Stealthily and with full determination it taught women to hide their intellect if they wished to be appreciated.

Ironically, on the set of the same film Monroe was discovered by a studio executive reading *The Autobiography of Lincoln Steffens.* Again she was admonished, this time because it was "dangerous to be seen reading such radical books in public."

In December of 1954, after the release of *There's No Business Like Show Business,* Marilyn Monroe left Hollywood for New York. "I don't want to play sex roles any more," she declared. "I just couldn't continue as a near-parody of sex." At least verbally, Monroe repudiated the image that had made her notorious, a statement that Mae West could never have made. West always sought autonomy by so exaggerating the sexuality which had made women objects that she became a virtual impersonation of the female.

†*Ibid.*, pp. 41-42.

Disguised in a black wig and dark glasses, clutching a plane ticket made out defiantly to "Zelda Zonk," Marilyn Monroe broke with the Hollywood that had created her. From the Monroe coyly cringing before condescending directors like Mankiewicz, she would become a woman who could greet an assistant director with the most graphic of four-letter words because he had interrupted her reading of Thomas Paine's *Rights of Man*.

The new Monroe began by breaking her contract with Twentieth Century-Fox. She refused to star in a follow-up to *How To Marry A Millionaire* called *How To Be Very, Very Popular*. She rejected outright the part of the mistress in *The Girl In The Red Velvet Swing* and that of the prostitute in *The Revolt of Mamie Stover*, just as she had earler refused to perform in *Pink Tights* as a schoolteacher who becomes a dancer on the Bowery. She underlined the seriousness of her aspirations by beginning study with Lee Strasberg and The Actors Studio where she mastered the principles of Stanislavsky. As Marlon Brando has proven, these precepts are aptly suited to film acting because in movies the actor must more often "be" or "behave" rather

THERE'S NO BUSINESS LIKE SHOW BUSINESS (1954). As Vicky

than intellectualize or analyze his part. Marilyn Monroe later described her experience with Strasberg from a similiar point of view: "...acting isn't something you do. Instead of doing it, it occurs...if you're going to start with logic, you might as well give up. You can have conscious preparation, but you must have unconscious results."*

At the Actors Studio Monroe acted the part of Blanche DuBois in Tennessee Williams' *Streetcar Named Desire* as well as Eugene O'Neill's Anna Christie. Later she attempted to realize an old aspiration by contracting to play Maugham's Sadie Thompson in a television production of *Rain*. The project never materialized because of her mental breakdown in 1961.

But in New York in 1954 a hopeful future lay before her. "I want good stories and good directors, and just not to be thrown into any old thing," said Marilyn. "I am a serious actress. I want to prove it." With a photographer named Milton Greene she formed her own production company, defying Fox, and she began to wait out a settlement. She told reporters, "I don't think I'll ever be through studying, so I want to live in New York where I'll be going to school."

When Fox eventually came to an agreement with Marilyn Monroe Productions, their contract stipulated that she would work only with a list of directors acceptable to her. This unusual agreement indicated that she was well aware that a director's talents largely determine the excellence of a film, and that too often an actor is only as good as the director. Those to whom Monroe was willing to entrust herself included John Ford, John Huston, David Lean, Billy Wilder, and Alfred Hitchcock.

Despite her enormous effort to break out of the mold in which Hollywood was determined to keep her, Marilyn Monroe only partly escaped the image which had catapulted her to fame. In one interview she attempted to describe "the method": "You think of things you've felt, people you've hated. We'll say you're half-conscious." But she became confused and concluded by saying, "Oh, my. I know I'm making this all sound stupid." There were moments when her self-possession, sense of purpose, and acceptance of herself were impressive. When she objected to a film story, a minor movie executive in New York reproved her: "I've been in this business thirty years and you're gonna tell me about it? What do you know?" She replied confidently, "I know only that I was born and that I'm still living. That's what I know."

*James Goode, *The Story of The Misfits* (New York, 1963), p. 203.

But for every triumph there were humiliations from the press and the industry, conniving until the last days of her life to keep her the dumb blonde they had packaged and sold as the ultimate sex symbol of the fifties. One reporter printed the malicious story that when he first met Marilyn Monroe, she was carrying a volume of Keats under her arm. He asked her if she were a Keats fan. Her supposed reply was, "I don't know... it's the right weight to balance on my head to learn to walk right." The remark is so incongruous one could be sure it was a fabrication if there were not also many stories of Marilyn collapsing into the role of "the girl" before the sneers of baiting reporters.

When Marilyn Monroe declared that, more than any other role, she wished to play Dostoevsky's Grushenka, a reporter nastily asked her to spell "Grushenka." Marilyn replied, "You can look it up in the book." When she went to England to make *The Prince And The Showgirl* with Laurence Olivier, she told the press that she liked Beethoven. Someone sardonically asked her which Beethoven pieces she preferred. She had to admit in defeat, and to all-knowing looks, "I know it when I hear it." Arthur Miller's friends would giggle when Marilyn mispronounced "Dostoevsky."

Marilyn's accounts of her humiliations at the hands of the press and others reveal a bewilderment and deep hurt. She never understood why her tormentors had so great a stake in presenting her as a mental incompetent:

> One woman asked me how long I thought a whale could remain submerged before it would die. Since I hadn't the faintest idea, and any guess I might make could look ridiculous in print, I asked her why she wanted me to answer such a strange question. "It's a kind of intelligence test," she said. I wondered whose intelligence was at stake—hers or mine.*

Even those directors who professed to like her personally were committed to portraying her as a person incapable of intelligence or rationality. One evening during a moment of relaxation on the set of *The Misfits*, Marilyn Monroe, gambling in a Reno watering spot with other members of the crew, asked John Huston what she should ask of the dice; "Don't think, honey," said Huston, "just throw. That's the story of your life. Don't think, do it."

The books she carried with her were counted by one reporter at two hundred. She kept a painting of Lincoln over her bed in New York and nearby a framed pho-

*Hedda Hopper, "Marilyn Monroe Tells The Truth to Hedda Hopper," *Photoplay* (January, 1953), p. 86.

tograph of Albert Einstein. She attended dramatic readings at the YMHA by Tennessee Williams. She made every possible effort to overcome the economic, social, and cultural deprivations of her childhood. She had an intense need to learn—a need far more sincere, genuine, and emotionally necessary to her than the glib pretensions of middle-brows who ridiculed her. But no matter what she did, Marilyn Monroe was insistently thought of as "the body."

In his play, *After The Fall*, written after her death, Arthur Miller would do nothing to dispel the favored image. But nowhere is the ugly complicity of the Hollywood studios and the press to sell this image of Marilyn more clearly revealed than in Douglas Watt's column in the *New York Daily News* on July 12, 1955. It was headlined "A Word Of Advice To A Poor Wandering Girl":

> And, this business with the Actors Studio, that training group for professional actors run by Elia Kazan—what are you doing there? You want to sound like Kim Stanley or Geraldine Page or somebody?... I'll bet that if you were to get up and walk across the room, the others would quit show business overnight.
>
> What it comes down to is this: you are throwing away your heritage. Worse than that, you are giving the brush to millions of red-blooded American boys for whom you have become a symbol of uncomplicated womanhood.

Given her overwhelming desire to be taken seriously as an artist, the orchestrated campaign of harassment and ridicule was calculated to drive her mad and destroy her, should she rebel against what the studios and the mass media had decreed her to be.

CHAPTER III.

A CRISIS OF IDENTITY

I fled from the tigers
I fled from the fleas
What got me at last—
mediocrities.

Bertolt Brecht. Dedicated to Marilyn Monroe by Viveca Lindfors.

The role of "star" was a fitting escape for Norma Jean Baker. In becoming another person—the dumb, vulnerable blonde with the whispery, accessible voice—she might earn the love forever denied the abandoned foster child, Norma Jean. Through her false persona she could hide the feelings which continued to possess her that her real self was unworthy and unlovable. As this fear and this defining emotion not only intensifed, but was re-enacted by the very screen persona designed to shield her, those early childhood feelings began to surface, causing pain and despair. It required countless doses of barbituates and heavy quantities of liquor (usually champagne or vodka) to kill the real self. Marilyn was in a double bind. She wanted to be in touch with her self, but the pain of her early years was too great. She had also sought the screen image as an escape from feeling valueless, but this image merely reinforced the original feelings of Norma Jean.

At the game of deception Hollywood had long been a master. Its aim, then as now, was to fabricate an antiseptic world inducing people to identify vicariously with characters either glamorous or heroic. It was a world without trauma in which the good win out. The audience was lulled and such dangerous realities as exploitation, social conflict and the destructiveness of established institutions were implicitly denied.

Threatened by the growing popularity of television as an alternative dream machine, the bankers who controlled the studios in the 1950s found in Marilyn Monroe an ideal soporific for audiences. She would exude sex and arouse lust in so childlike a manner that women as well as men could respond. She was ultimately unthreatening.

The loneliness of the girl Marilyn, obsessed with denying the needs of Norma Jean and fearful of discovering her true feelings, led her to drift into a variety of dependent relationships. Unconsciously she reasoned that if she relinquished the need to make judgments of her own, Norma Jean could be obliterated.

Constantly present with Marilyn Monroe on the set, through the first half of her career, was dramatic coach Natasha Lytess, whom

HOW TO MARRY A MILLIONAIRE (1953). A multiplicity of Marilyns

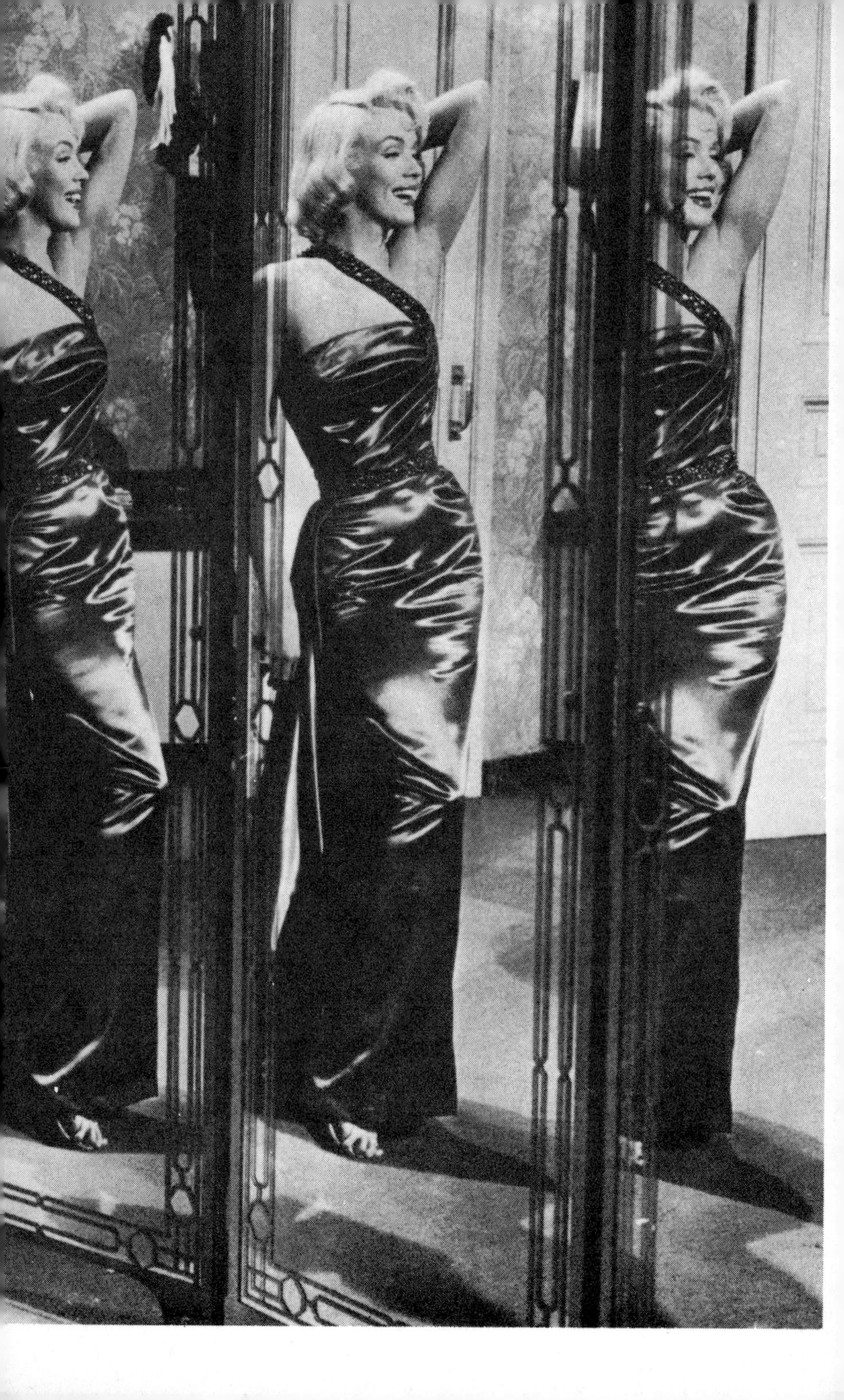

Marilyn met at Columbia before her first real film role in *Ladies of the Chorus*. When they met in the late forties, Lytess said that Marilyn was so unsure of herself that she was "unable even to take refuge in her own insignificance." Later Lytess was replaced by the omnipresent figure of Paula Strasberg.

Marilyn Monroe's terror on film sets, which became legendary, was caused by the fact that acting itself, reaching for deep feelings, as the Stanislavsky method demanded, inevitably summoned the real self. In Marilyn's case this meant the rejected Norma Jean who, she felt, must have been inadequate and unworthy or her father and mother would not have abandoned her. These feelings produced another, that she could not hope to perform well, that success, like love, must remain forever elusive.

The need to escape from this specter drove Marilyn Monroe to the telephone. Her compulsive calls to all and sundry were appeals for help as well as an enactment of her quest for parental love, and these calls involved countless hours weekly. It was this Marilyn Monroe who wrote poetry about the dissociation of self in which life was something to escape, its needs repressed to the end:

> Help Help
> Help I feel life coming closer
> When all I want is to die.

There were two Marilyn Monroes—the public personality with wet lips sensuously parted and the private Marilyn whose facial expression and voice were entirely different from those of the Hollywood star. There were two selves as well, the conscious and the unconscious, the willed and the real. Aware of being alienated from her deepest self, she lacked all confidence. After a take she would often rush up to Miss Lytess for approval: "Was I all right? Did I do it the way you wanted me to?" She was beset by fears she never understood and wrote in her notebook, "What am I afraid of? I know I can act. But I'm afraid. And I shouldn't be, mustn't be."

She was notoriously late on the set, sometimes arriving at 6:00 P.M. for a morning call, but she did not lack insight. "Being late," she explained, "is a desire not to be there and it's a desire that has something to do with my fears."

When she was due at the studio, she would take long baths instead, perceiving the bath as an attempt to wash away the facade. She described these baths as a compulsion to return to being Norma Jean, to allow her psyche to surface briefly. While she was bathing, she dreamed of retribution and felt solace. She would speak of her two selves with detachment, as if

GENTLEMEN PREFER BLONDES (1953)
As Loreli

describing her feelings might assuage them:

> It isn't Marilyn Monroe in the tub, but Norma Jean. I'm giving Norma Jean a treat. She used to have to bathe in water used by six or eight other people. Now she can bathe in water as clean and transparent as a pane of glass. And it seems that Norma Jean can't get enough of fresh bath water that smells of real perfume.
>
> People are eager to see me. And I remember the years I was unwanted. All the hundreds of times nobody wanted to see the little servant girl, Norma Jean, not even her mother. I feel a queer satisfaction in punishing the people who are wanting me now. But it's not them I'm really punishing. It's the long-ago people who didn't want Norma Jean . . . the later I am, the happier Norma Jean grows.*

Although they border on self-pity, her reflections express her longing to be whole and at peace with herself. Many years of psychoanalytic therapy gave her insight but little relief. She continued to wish for love which could never be retrieved, for the early love without which the child's ego could neither grow strong nor flourish.

*Quoted by Maurice Zolotow, *Marilyn Monroe* (New York, 1960), pp. 152-153.

Publicity pose

Throughout her life, Marilyn Monroe waged the battles of the infant Norma Jean. She could not fully experience or believe in herself as an adult woman, and this awareness undermined her as the serious, hard-working actress she also needed to be. After an early success in *Gentlemen Prefer Blondes,* she felt the split in her personality, a divided self neither half of which she could truly feel was real: "I feel as though it's all happening to someone right next to me. I'm close—I can feel it, I can hear it, but it isn't really *me.*"

This split between early feelings and consciousness underlay her prolonged crisis of identity as Norma Jean versus Marilyn or sex symbol versus serious actress. She could not commit herself to either of these roles for long. Marilyn in New York, the declared serious performer, saw the press with a new voice—clear, forceful, and direct. She was neither shy nor did she play dumb. Unlike the Hollywood Marilyn, she spoke loudly so that she could be heard.

Yet when she appeared on Edward R. Murrow's *Person To*

Person, she insisted on wearing a tight skirt and sweater, although she had been requested to wear a full skirt to conceal the microphone which would be placed on her body. In a restaurant when someone told her, "You seem to be lunching with a lot of men today," she gave the expected, wide-eyed response: "Yes, isn't it wonderful?" She played up to her vapid image with such comments as "I don't mind this being a man's world—as long as I can be a woman in it."

Thus Marilyn Monroe gave in to the very demands she had learned to transcend. *Life* photographer Philippe Halsman commented that "the only way she knew to get herself accepted was to make herself desired." She would resort to her role as sex symbol even when in the next breath she spoke of her aspirations to be a serious actress: "I want to be an artist, not a freak."

Because the needs of Norma Jean were permanently unresolved, Marilyn Monroe reverted repeatedly to advertising the body which had first brought her success and transformed her from Norma Jean to Marilyn. As a child, she had wished to be "so beautiful that people would turn to look at me as I passed." She had impulses to appear naked in church, to throw off her identity as the foundling Norma Jean, even as in adulthood she would pose nude at times and appear in the nude in films as varied as *Niagara* and *Bus Stop*. Her nudity, both in childhood fantasy and adult life, was an appeal to be loved for herself.

"I used to play-act all the time," Marilyn Monroe said of her childhood. "For one thing, it meant I could live in a more interesting world than the one around me." Although the adult Marilyn wished sincerely and consciously "to have people comment on my fine dramatic performances," she had also to cater to the whims of the unsatisfied Norma Jean and continue to be limited in the same ways as the uneducated Norma Jean was limited.

Thus we can understand her rationalizations and the seeming contradictions abounding in her person. "If you are born with what the world calls sex appeal," she once said, "you can either let it wreck you or use it to your advantage." At the end of her life she was still trying to reconcile two opposites, her role as sex symbol *par excellence* and the need to express the consciously felt truths of a mature, sensitive woman. "That's the trouble," said Marilyn, "a sex symbol becomes a thing—I just hate to be a thing." Yet the next moment she went on to add, "but if I'm going to be a symbol of something, I'd rather have it sex."

Like a pendulum she accepted

and then rejected sex parts. She would do *The Seven Year Itch* but not *Pink Tights*. After her declaration of independence and year of exile in New York, she returned to Hollywood for *Bus Stop* to play, again, the dumb blonde. All the while she struggled for autonomy as a film actress in a medium largely governed by the artistic competence of the director:

> "They tell you to cry one tear, and if you feel two and therefore cry two, it's no good. If you change "the" to "a" in your lines, they correct you. An actress is not a machine, but they treat you like one. A money machine."*

The same woman could declare, after the failure of her marriage to Arthur Miller, "I have too many fantasies to be a housewife . . . I guess I am a fantasy." Alvah Bessie invents one of her film lines in *The Symbol*, a trashy novel based on Marilyn Monroe's life: "I'm *nobody's* private party—not even my own."

Toward the end of her life the dissociation of sensibility became too painful to bear. She spoke of "beginning to look at things—really look. To find the real inside center of me—and then to look out at the world in a new way." It was, perhaps, too late because the pain she fought to allay induced such quantities of barbituates and alcohol that the damage was becoming irreversible.

There was great resilience in the personality of Marilyn Monroe. Without it she could not have come as far as she had or have held out during the long years in Hollywood scrounging for bit parts. But her internal injury won out in the end. She had kept too little for herself. In her need to win love, she gave herself away in sympathy and generosity. It left her depleted of reserves for the times when loneliness and terror would drive her to ever greater doses of Nembutal.

This was the same Marilyn who recognized her working-class origins, who was undisturbed by the Communist and radical affiliations of members of the Actors' Lab because "they're for the people, aren't they?" It was the Marilyn who supported Arthur Miller during the witch hunt and who would even be elected as an alternate delegate to the Connecticut State Democratic Convention in 1960.

It was Marilyn in quest of being a "real" person. And it was also the Marilyn who, beside a tousled and completely unglamorous photograph in which she looked as if she had just awakened from sleep, wrote in an album she made for a friend's birthday, "This is my favorite." It represented Norma Jean. Her lips, rare for a photograph of Marilyn Monroe, are closed; her

*"The Real Marilyn," *Ms.* (August 1972), p.38.

smile is pensive, half-serious. There is no trace of sexiness. "I don't look at myself as a commodity," said Marilyn Monroe late in her life, "but I'm sure a lot of people have." In her last and much-quoted interview she begged the reporter to accept seriously and with empathy her struggle to unite the divided elements of her self, to find wholeness and clear purpose:

> Please don't make me a joke. End the interview with what I believe....I don't mind making jokes, but I don't like being looked at as one. I want to be an artist—an actress with integrity. My work is the only ground I've ever had to stand on. I seem to have a whole superstructure with no foundation—but I'm working on the foundation.*

Only a thoughtful and honest person could describe herself with such insight, but Marilyn Monroe found callous indifference far more often than she encountered compassion.

The superstructure had been imposed on the ambitious young Marilyn Monroe by a movie industry in which commercial considerations were paramount. Since the 1930s, it has produced little of artistic merit in the history of cinema. Such a world could only drive a young woman longing to define herself as an intelligent actress to the very insanity that Marilyn Monroe had dreaded all her life as her heritage. It reinforced the loneliness she felt within her own divided self.

On one occasion, after she left Hollywood for New York, Marilyn Monroe sketched in charcoal a little black girl with one stocking up and the other down. She entitled it "lonely." The black girl represented the outcast Norma Jean whose spirit haunted Marilyn Monroe throughout her short life, and from whose hurt and trauma she was never able to recover.

*See "The Real Marilyn," *Ms* (August 1972), P. 42 and Alan Levy, "A Good Long Look At Myself," *Marilyn Monroe: A Composite View*, ed. Edward Wagenknecht (Philadelphia, 1969), p. 36.

CHAPTER IV

THE MEN IN HER LIFE

"Teach me, Quentin, I don't know how to be."
Maggie in Arthur Miller's AFTER THE FALL.

Marilyn Monroe was married three times and knew many men. The mysterious last man in her life, a political figure, was described by columnists as possessing a large family, and a man as prominent as either herself or DiMaggio in his day. Throughout her adult life Marilyn sought in men a means of relieving her pain, a panacea that would lift the burden of her life from her shoulders.

She longed for a strong and caring father who would protect her. Like the women she played in her films, she lived in the belief that such men could make up for the hurts and losses she had suffered as Norma Jean. As late as the year of her death, she said that she "like[d] men more than women, I guess it's Freudian. I trust men more than women, inevitably." And throughout her life whenever she spoke to the press she mentioned her need of "a man, marriage, a home, children." That she had corrective surgery in 1959 to enable her to have children after two miscarriages testified to her sincerity.

As a starlet struggling for success in a ruthless Hollywood, Marilyn Monroe, like other young women of similar attributes, had many opportunities to exchange sex for parts in films, even for bit parts. Yet Marilyn repeatedly asserted that she refused and her years of difficulty before she made *The Asphalt Jungle* and *All About Eve* in 1949 bear out her words. "I was never kept, to be blunt about it," she said. "I always kept myself. I have always had a pride in the fact that I was on my own." Her denial that she was the mistress of Joseph Schenck, the scion of Twentieth Century-Fox, was undoubtedly truthful. Despite his enormous power in Hollywood, he was never instrumental in her receiving a single part.

Marilyn's first husband was a young factory worker named Jim Dougherty. When she was sixteen, her guardian Grace McKee Goddard insistently arranged the marriage shortly before her move to West Virginia. Her own husband had already fondled Norma Jean more than intimately and it was considered "impractical" for her to move with the family.

Even from his own accounts of the marriage, Doughterty emerges as a narrow-minded, rather closed young man. He was extremely jealous of his young wife, especially

Marilyn testing for first movie, SCUDDA HOO! SCUDDA HAY! (1948). She was cut from film.

after they moved to Catalina Island. Dougherty himself remembers Marilyn as a "wonderful housekeeper who darned socks and sewed on buttons like a veteran housewife." He denied out of pride Marilyn's story that she was raped at the age of nine, declaring that Marilyn was a virgin when they married. Nor does he mention his own jealousy that obliged her to remain one day on the outside porch while she talked to his best-friend because she feared an invitation to enter the house would stir her husband's wrath.

Dougherty has told how Marilyn always addressed him as "Dearest Daddy," signing her love notes, "Your baby." He has also presented Marilyn as stupid as the women she has played in her films. He describes her wandering in the street in her nightgown and on another occasion nearly driving their car into a streetcar. He has her throwing a pot of coffee at a spark from a shorted wire beneath the carpet and even attempting to bring a cow out of the rain into the house. Righteously he claims to have told her that she could have "one career only." Long after their days together, when he had remarried, he proudly pointed out that "all four females in my house are content to stay on board and let me steer their ship."

But such an atmosphere must

have been insufferable for a young woman. Marilyn took the occasion of his absence during the war to take a job as a paint sprayer in a factory and then, when the opportunity arose, as a model. She recalls that she and Dougherty hardly spoke to each other. It is also probable that the actual divorce was precipitated by the fact that studios at that time would not hire a married starlet in fear of her possible pregnancy. In any case, Marilyn preferred the insecurity of determining her own life, without a man if need be.

Her second major attachment was to Johnny Hyde, executive vice-president of the William Morris Agency. Hyde was the person most responsible for her rise to stardom and for her parts in *The Asphalt Jungle* and *All About Eve*. He left his wife and four sons for Marilyn and was a man far older than she, with a heart condition that would severely shorten his life. Marrying him, as he urged her to do, meant that she would become a very rich widow before long and she knew it. Yet Marilyn refused. She did not love Johnny Hyde, although she was enormously grateful to him.

Marilyn's most celebrated marriage was to Joe DiMaggio, a man who could provide a silent strength, but who had little capacity to assuage her fears or help her to achieve an identity. Significantly, her wedding gift to DiMaggio was the nude transparencies rejected for the famous calendar because they exposed the pelvic region.

DiMaggio's marathon television-watching became famous. Marilyn would serve his dinner on a small folding table while he kept his eyes glued to the set. She told her friend, columnist Sidney Skolsky: "I never say, oh, gee, I want to see such-and-such a program." If Marilyn had looked to DiMaggio for the strong father who would comfort the foundling Norma Jean, enabling her to grow as Marilyn, she was disappointed. When he became angry, DiMaggio would retreat into silence. He was always ill at ease with the image Marilyn Monroe presented to the world. His distaste as Marilyn filmed the skirt-blowing scene in *The Seven Year Itch* was visible to all.

Before their nine-month marriage had ended, Marilyn began returning home late at night and seeing the friends with whom DiMaggio was uncomfortable, friends he later accused of responsibility for her death. But when Marilyn learned of his involvement with another woman, she took an overdose of sleeping pills in his presence and he had to call a doctor. It has been said that she also attempted suicide during her marriage to Dougherty.

The pattern is clear. To punish these men for not loving her enough, while simultaneously appealing for care, Marilyn threatened to end her life. Most of the time she "knew" that rescue was imminent, even as she had married these men in order to be rescued from the plight of a divided self. For the ravaged Norma Jean there was never enough love because its very presence heightened the early feeling of deprivation. Her most ambitious candidate for rescuer, a knight in creative armor who could answer the need for dignity experienced by the uneducated, unloved Norma Jean, was Arthur Miller.

They had met for the first time in 1950 on the set of *As Young As You Feel.* She confided to him that she longed for someone to admire since she had never had a father. He suggested that she read Sandburg's books about Abraham Lincoln. They corresponded and met over the next years, although they did not marry until 1956. On the back of her wedding picture, Marilyn wrote "hope, hope, hope." Through marriage, especially to a man of artistic and intellectual attainment like Miller, she hoped to liberate herself vicariously from deeply felt inadequacy. To match her beige wedding dress, she dyed her white bridal veil in coffee, an anxious act foreshadowing her collapse as a potentially serious actress and mature woman, which occurred during her marriage to Miller.

As in the case of the stolid, non-intellectual DiMaggio, she wished to shelter in the protection of a self-sufficient man certain of his place in the world. Occasionally she would deprecate herself in the effort to create the necessity for Miller to take care of her, even when this need was not externally apparent. Thus she described a room in her New York apartment with Miller: "This room is mostly my idea, or maybe my fault, because my husband let me do what I wanted with it."

Marilyn Monroe even attempted to obliterate her identity as a screen personality. She told reporters that she bought all Miller's shirts, socks and ties, and personally took care of his laundry: "I definitely don't approve when a man has to go out and he has no clean shirts to wear because his wife has been out playing bridge." The statement is striking because it is so reminiscent of the Norma Jean married to Jim Dougherty, whose assumed role was that of housekeeper, rather than that of the serious actress who could easily hire others to attend to domestic chores or, at the very least, share the essential tasks with her husband.

With Arthur Miller

The marriage could not hope to succeed with Marilyn so unable to carry the burden of her identity and so quick to regress to the quest for a strong, loving father who would assume total care and solve all her problems. Immediately after her marriage to Miller, she said, "A man should be allowed to do his work, and a woman should know when he wants to relax." She appeared almost amnesiac, as if she had forgotten completely her earlier passionately avowed aspirations. She told reporters that she enjoyed being just a wife. She expressed pride in her ability to bake bread and make homemade noodles. Having converted to Judaism, she displayed a cultivated talent for preparing Jewish specialties like borscht and gefülte fish.

As had DiMaggio, if less explicitly, Miller demanded the quiet and privacy of marriage to an ordinary woman without an independent career. At the same time both men craved possession of the glamorous blonde movie star. Caught between the desire to be taken seriously as a human being, which she felt possible only through the autonomy of a profession, and the incompatible demands of her husbands, Marilyn felt acutely the absence of peace and stability which she had sought. In the early days with Miller she spoke of the "peace of mind" the marriage brought her and, with considerable humility and self-denial, of their relation as that between "pupil" and "teacher."

Long having written himself out (as his mediocre work of the 1960s and early 1970s amply reveals), Miller spent more and more time with Marilyn on the sets of her films, helping her choose still photographs and paste clippings in scrapbooks. In London, when he felt the fatigue of being a "hanger-on" in her life, she asked him, "Why are you getting involved in this?"

Just as she had brought her needs to him, Miller equally used Marilyn to fill a void in his own life. On the set of *The Misfits* with their marriage clearly over, Miller met his next wife, Inge Morath, a Magnum photographer assigned to the film. Marilyn and Miller at one point emerged from their hotel to tell reporters, "We're going out for a walk, just like everyday people."

The need or obligation to pretend to be "everyday people" was as much a Hollywood fiction as the screen characters Marilyn Monroe portrayed. Miller's insistent demand that such a life was desirable for Monroe proved destructive to the real and growing possibility that she would win her struggle to fulfill herself as an actress.

After Marilyn Monroe's death, Arthur Miller wrote a play called

On the set of THE MISFITS with director John Huston and Arthur Miller

After The Fall which dissected their marriage. Apart from a selectively cruel anatomy of Marilyn, it is an apologia for his own sterile and unproductive life after early success. The character of Quentin, Miller's alter ego, is bathetic in his attempt to justify his own failures. "These goddamned women have injured me," he declaims, as if Miller's two bad marriages could account for his inadequacies as a serious writer. Just as Maggie clearly represents Monroe, there is little distance, ironic or otherwise, between Miller and Quentin.

So that there would be no doubt of Maggie's identity, Miller had Barbara Loden use Marilyn's own private wigmaker. Her wardrobes were imitated, and Miller made a point of ensuring that Marilyn's gestures were correctly imitated. The result is a portrayal of Marilyn as a vindictive demon, when she is not insane or mindlessly stupid. Marilyn pleaded with interviewers not to "make her a joke." Miller's Maggie calls herself "a joke to most people." She constantly says "s'cuze me" and is leeringly solicitous and grateful for the male lust she incites.

Many of Marilyn's famous quotes are there to add credibility to the imputed incompetence and foolish blind trust with which Miller characterizes her. Maggie oafishly leaves all her money to a conniving agent, and Miller presents her in general as a whore: "She had been chewed and spat out by a long line of grinning men! Her name floating in the stench of locker rooms and parlor-car cigar smoke!" Quentin's noble task is to grace her with dignity, to provide a screen for her profligacy, alcoholism and drug addiction, but above all, her stupidity. The play confirms the task as hopeless, even as Miller coldly commented on the inevitability of her demise shortly after her death.

Every fault attributable to a woman Miller lays at Marilyn's door. He renders her jealous of his mother because that lady had said that Maggie was putting on weight. She is careless with money and, above all, cynically addicted to fake suicides which she stages solely to test the subordinate loyalty of her consort. Destructively she tears her husband from his work. In a stream of invective, Miller strips Marilyn of all the mitigating experiences which she had disclosed in seeking understanding for her inadequacies and problems:

> If you could only say, I have been kicked around, but I have been just as inexcusably vicious to others; I have called my husband idiot in public, I have been utterly selfish despite my generosity, I have been hurt by a long line of men but I have cooperated with my persecutors.

And in a paroxysm of self-righteousness and inflated prose, Quentin enjoins her to "Do the hardest thing of all—see your own hatred, and live!"

In a solitary moment of truth about himself, Miller includes the painful incident of Marilyn discovering his lack of feeling for her expressed in his diary, which he left conspicuously open in their London house during the shooting of *The Prince And The Showgirl*. In the play what Maggie discovers are words which reveal something of Miller's own psychology: "The only one I will ever love is my daughter." In Marilyn Monroe's own account, Miller wrote in the diary that he had once thought her to be an "angel" (as Bo thinks of her in *Bus Stop*), but that he had been wrong. She had hurt him, the entry continues, far more than had his first wife. If Olivier, the diary continues, was beginning to think of her as a troublesome bitch, Miller no longer had a decent answer to that one.

His contriving for Marilyn to discover his loss of feeling so impersonally is clear evidence of cowardice and cruelty. But in *After The Fall* the callousness is projected onto its victim. It is Quentin who accuses *Maggie* of trying to kill *him* by making him feel guilty for her life while simultaneously wanting him for her rescuer. Miller's willingness to write so hostile an interpretation of his wife's character and life shortly after her death speaks volumes. Even if the unnuanced details of "Maggie's" personality were a summary of Marilyn Monroe, the play is unfeeling, overly protested special pleading.

Miller would not attend the funeral of Marilyn, while Joe DiMaggio, who had suffered equally from the public exposure imposed by marriage to so difficult a personality, made all the arrangements, whispering "I love you" three times at her tomb. In happier moments Miller described a Marilyn no feature of whom is present in his shrewish portrayal of Maggie: "She has a tremendous native feeling. She has more guts than a slaughterhouse. Being with her, people want not to die. She's all woman, the most womanly woman in the world." There are few antecedents in the history of literature in which an author maligned the memory of a former love so explicitly and relentlessly. It is an action of which Marilyn Monroe was never capable.

During the waning days of her marriage to Arthur Miller, Marilyn had a brief affair with the French actor, Yves Montand, whom she wished to marry. Montand's recollections of Marilyn are infinitely less jaundiced than those of Miller. He describes her as "an enchanting child . . . a simple girl without any guile." He regrets his inability to sustain a relationship she very much desires because he is firmly committed to his wife, Simone Signoret. He casts no blame. Montand allows that had she been sophisticated "none of this ever would have happened," concluding that although she is a world figure, "she is still a child."

Montand's remarks about Marilyn Monroe betray both condescension and self-justification, as if the responsibility for their relationship were hers alone. But this aside, Montand felt evident tenderness for her. His assessment of Marilyn on the set of *Let's Make Love,* in which they co-starred, was that she was "honest," "generous," "a lovely, gifted, and amusing woman." It is only a shame that Miller could not have found within himself a commensurate compassion when their relationship had ended. While a brief affair is not a marriage, Miller's meanness of spirit ultimately passes harsher judgment on him than on the woman so eager for real affection whom he publicly excoriated once she was dead.

CHAPTER V

THE FILMS

"She was so young and pretty, so shy and nervous on that picture, but I remember the scene where she was supposed to be sunning in the backyard of the apartment house we all lived in. When Marilyn walked on the set in her bathing suit and walked to the beach chair, the whole crew gasped, gaped, and seemed to turn to stone. They just stopped work and stared; Marilyn had that electric something...."

June Haver recalling the shooting of LOVE NEST.

Not one of Marilyn Monroe's films is significant as film art—with the possible exception of Mankiewicz's *All About Eve*, which achieved some caché because of its camp and the presence of Bette Davis. No one, however, has suggested that *All About Eve* enlarges the potential of the medium. In all these films, Marilyn Monroe caricatures herself. In *Don't Bother To Knock* it is her fear of insanity; *Some Like It Hot* treats her alcoholism; her self-consciousness as an actress is so apparent that it almost becomes a theme of *River Of No Return*. Most often she is the natural if slightly vacuous blonde of *The Seven Year Itch*, who decides to soak her sheets and pillowcases in ice water to escape the heat, but changes her mind because "that's too icky."

When Marilyn Monroe was asked about her part in *The Prince And The Showgirl*, she replied, "I play a human being." Asked the same question about *The Misfits*, she answered, "I play a girl." It is true that her screen character is always raw and "feminine," more a life-force than a fully realized and conscious personality. One has only to compare her parts with those of Anne Baxter (Eve), Bette Davis (Margo), or even Celeste Holm (Karen) in *All About Eve*. Given the image created for Marilyn Monroe long before she became a star, the studios found it inconceivable to consider her for the part of Eve, rather than that of the brainless but conniving starlet, Miss Caswell.

She achieved such great fame and notoriety that she became a household word, and, as she feared, a national "joke." But despite this "importance," virtually all her films centered on the psychology and perceptions of male characters for whom she served as a foil, and frequently a prize for their success at being masculine in the crass Hollywood sense. This is even true of *The Misfits*, a film designed expressly for Marilyn by her then husband, Arthur Miller.

The Prince And The Showgirl,

Early portrait

despite being the first project of her independent company, Marilyn Monroe Productions, pivots around the Regent, played by Laurence Olivier. He is a man who has lost the ability to feel, but who is restored to love by the showgirl, Elsie Marina. *Some Like It Hot* is about two musicians, played by Jack Lemmon and Tony Curtis, who disguise themselves as women and join an all-girl band to escape from the underworld. Most of the humor of the film derives from their antics. In the second half of the film, with the exception of the scene on the yacht, Marilyn is scarcely present at all.

Bus Stop, the film which many critics have argued contains her best screen performance, is primarily about Bo Decker who reluctantly learns to respect a woman rather than regard her as a head of cattle. Bo's farcical actions and come-uppance lie at the heart of the film. Marilyn plays Cherie, his "angel," whose insistence on respect (paralleling her real-life need) transforms Bo from brash adolescent to budding adult.

Despite her financial value to whatever project she joined, Monroe was never allowed the part of a character capable of growth or change or one whose intelligence and sensibility carried or determined the action of the film. Even *Don't Bother To Knock*, the mediocre film she made early in her career, has her playing a psychotic baby sitter for whom the male lead, played by Richard Widmark, accomplishes the resolution of all difficulties. In few of her films was Marilyn Monroe allowed a chance to play the kind of person whom she wished to become in her private life.

More perniciously than for any other star of her time, Monroe was given an incredibly narrow range of roles with which to work. All involved a sexy, naïve, unintentionally funny blonde who drove men to wild acts. These were sometimes in fantasy as in *The Seven Year Itch* and sometimes in reality as with the murderous husband (Joseph Cotten) in *Niagara*. It was an image too lascivious for television—which is why she appeared there only once, quite early in her career, as a guest on "The Jack Benny Show."

The function of the Monroe image was also a presentation of the "ideal" woman whose life centers around a man. She remains incomplete unless she is with a man who can dominate her and whom, therefore, she can respect—as Kay learns to value Matt Calder (Robert Mitchum) in *River of No Return*. In none of her films does she play a woman capable of rationality, interesting thought, or a productive or creative life.

BUS STOP (1956). As Cherie

In *Dangerous Years*, her second film, she played a waitress, even as she was an ex-waitress in her first major film, *Niagara.* Most often she is a music-hall or saloon entertainer. This is true of *Gentlemen Prefer Blondes, There's No Business Like Show Business, All About Eve, River Of No Return, The Prince and The Showgirl, Bus Stop, Let's Make Love,* and *Some Like It Hot,* as well as *Ladies of the Chorus.* And as an entertainer what she has to sell is never talent, but unnuanced sex appeal, and the most obvious capacity to arouse.

Frequently she is working class and unskilled, fulfilling Hollywood's myth that those uneducated and of the lower classes are richer in animal sexuality than those less bound by poverty and cultural disadvantage. (This alone would undermine Marilyn Monroe herself as a woman of poor origins.) In her films other women pale beside Marilyn—Jean Peters in *Niagara,* Evelyn Keyes in *The Seven Year Itch* and Hope Lange in *Bus Stop.* This occurs because part of the myth has it that the woman who is possessed solely of instinct and sheer naked appeal will fare far better than those who offer intelligence, humor or the aspiration to be more than the subordinate of a man.

With rare exceptions like *Niagara,* Marilyn on screen is virtuous at heart, although like Cherie in *Bus Stop,* circumstances have forced her into misadventures. The most typical of the Marilyn personae is the girl in *The Seven Year Itch* who tempts, but who is rather glad when a man is married and committed so that her kind heart need not suffer the unpleasantness of refusing his advances. Hollywood had it both ways. She was overtly titillating, but ultimately coy and devoid of real sexual intent. This was the desired image of women—tantalizing but themselves asexual, except as providers of pleasure.

Most of these women are at odds with life, adrift, like Kay in *River Of No Return,* Roslyn, in *The Misfits,* or Cherie in *Bus Stop.* When they are on their own, they make the wrong choices. They are bored and dissatisfied. Their lives are changed and made viable by the appearance of an attractive, eligible man, whether he is Clark Gable, Yves Montand, Don Murray or Robert Mitchum. In some of the earlier films even a cloddish David Wayne would do.

The first of Marilyn's thirty screen roles was a cheap imitation *State Fair* vehicle for one of Twentieth Century-Fox's blonde stars, June Haver. Monroe was billed only as a "girlfriend" of the star. In a canoe, she and Colleen Townsend paddle past Robert Karnes

DANGEROUS YEARS (1948). With Donald Curtis

who is fishing and then wave "hello" when they see June Haver. The "one line" of dialogue wound up on the cutting-room floor and all that remained of Marilyn in *Scudda Hoo! Scudda Hay!* (1948) was an extreme long shot of two girls in a canoe.

In her second film, *Dangerous Years* (1948), she had a bit part as a waitress named "Eve" in a teenage haunt. It was one of the "juvenile delinquency" pictures common to the fifties, when the first indications of youth disaffection with the ills of society began to disturb Hollywood. Monroe wore a uniform, dark-red lipstick fashionable at the time, and long golden hair, similar to her hairstyle in the famous nude calendar. After these two "roles," she was dropped by Twentieth Century-Fox, but at Columbia she won second billing in a predictable film called *Ladies of the Chorus* (1948).

Marilyn was teamed with Adele Jergens, who played her mother, and who was kept by Columbia when the film was finished, while Marilyn was dropped. This alone indicates, if did nothing else, the absurdity of a star system in which, as on a slave block, traders bid for the best flesh and reject what they deem less exploitable.

LADIES OF THE CHORUS (1948). With Rand Brooks and Adele Jergens

LADIES OF THE CHORUS (1948). Marilyn in center

The plot centers around an aging chorus girl (Jergens) whose marriage to a wealthy young man was annulled by his elite family because of her unseemly profession and poor origins. Her daughter (Marilyn), now finds herself pursued by Randy Carroll (Rand Brooks), just such a rich idle man with a snobbish family. Marilyn's mother opposes the marriage on the ground that her daughter will also be used and then discarded. In the end Randy's mother improbably pretends that she, too, was once a "lady of the chorus" to win her society friends to an acceptance of chorus girl Marilyn as her son's bride. Not all the "better people" have class prejudice and a poor young stripper may indeed hope to catch a rich and eligible man. When Bubbles, the star, quits in the middle of a performance, Marilyn goes on in her place singing, inanely, "Anyone can see I love you." She is very thin, her lips dark red, her hair permanent-waved à la Rita Hayworth, then Columbia's top star. The famous Monroe bosom is nowhere visible.

Marilyn's best number in the film was "Every Baby Needs A Da-Da-Daddy" ("to keep her free ... if he hasn't got a million, then a half will do"). It epitomized the image of women to which Monroe was herself thoroughly assimilated in her career, and neatly linked passivity to gold-digging dependence. The song, of course, reminds one of Marilyn's nickname for Dougherty. The Da-Da-Daddy number was spliced into Columbia's *Okinawa* (1952), where it was viewed by men on a troop ship. The final refrain, "Could my Da-Da-Daddy be you?" provides the motivation for the rest of the film.

When Marilyn is invited to stay at the Carroll household, her manner becomes demure, pliable and unsure. Her uplifted chin imparts innocence and the film now presents the coy side of the female. Beneath the alluring burlesque façade she is not *really* a "lady of the chorus," but a lady-in-waiting for the right young man who will take care of her and bring her riches and comfort to match her natural sweetness.

The film is a Grade C potboiler, although it possesses the same values as more skillful films. It gave Marilyn her first chance, and if it revealed nothing else, it convinced the studios that she was highly photogenic.

Marilyn's next film role was in *Love Happy* with the Marx Brothers. Her part consisted of one gag with Groucho. In the film, he plays a private detective and she a would-be client. He asks what he can do for her and she complains that men keep following her all the time. She then slinks off in the inimitable, undulating walk which became notorious with *Niagara*.

After the tour for *Love Happy* (1950), which as an impoverished starlet she felt she couldn't refuse, Marilyn took another small role with even less dialogue. She played a chorus girl in a *A Ticket To Tomahawk* (1950). She wore a yellow satin, mini-skirted affair with puffed sleeves, so typical of the forties. Her small role was crudely suggestive and her only line was "Hmmmm." But in the musical number, "Oh, What A Forward Young Man You Are," which she and three other women do with Dan Dailey, she is the most striking, youthful, and vibrant of them all, and she seems to be the one Dailey favors. The Monroe smile is radiant and, in retrospect, unmistakable.

Monroe became a screen personality, if not yet a "star," with two films released in 1950. Both parts came to her with the aid of Johnny Hyde and in both she had roles that would stereotype her for the remainder of her career. In *The Asphalt Jungle* she portrayed the

LOVE HAPPY (1950). With Groucho Marx

A TICKET TO TOMAHAWK (1950). Marilyn at extreme right. With Dan Dailey

beautiful blonde mistress of a crooked lawyer played by Louis Calhern.

Because Marilyn had rehearsed reclining when she read the lines, and no couch was available when she tested for Huston, she asked if she could do the part on the floor. Huston agreed. Foreshadowing the attitude she would take throughout her career, Marilyn insisted on a second run-through even though she had been told she won the part on the first.

One has only to compare *Asphalt Jungle* with *The Misfits* to measure the change resulting from competition from television and foreign films in Hollywood from the early to the late fifties. In *The Asphalt Jungle,* Marilyn had to be called the "niece" of Calhern. In *The Misfits* her affair with Gay Langland (Gable) is presented as completely natural, in no way necessitating either moralizing or concealment.

Throughout *The Asphalt Jungle*, Angela (Marilyn) calls Calhern "Uncle," although he doesn't like it. She yawns and stretches, enticing him; she pulls away when he grabs her. In the big scene in which she betrays Calhern to the police by denying his alibi, she is

THE ASPHALT JUNGLE (1950). With Pat Flaherty

THE ASPHALT JUNGLE (1950). On the set with director John Huston

childish to the point of being simple-minded as she runs through the apartment to show him an ad for her hoped-for trip to Cuba. Mindless, she is enthusiastic only about the virtues of a green bathing suit over a white one. Her favorite word is "yipes," and she is an easy mark for the policeman with whom she mindlessly flirts when he urges her to betray Calhern.

Her big daddy, Calhern, has lost his power. Alone and frightened, she admits that he was not with her on the night of the murder. Her face is contorted with confusion, as if the events are too complex for her feeble mind. The parting shots go to Calhern who tells her, "You did pretty well, considering." He urges her not to worry because she'll have "plenty of trips," at least as long as she remains young, beautiful, and up for the highest bid.

THE ASPHALT JUNGLE (1950). With Louis Calhern

ALL ABOUT EVE (1950). With (left to right) Gregory Ratoff, Anne Baxter, Gary Merrill, George Sanders, and Celeste Holm

Marilyn's role in *All About Eve* was similar. This time she is the mistress of critic Addison DeWitt (George Sanders) and as an ambitious would-be actress is referred to as his "protégée." Her name is "Miss Caswell," and DeWitt sarcastically introduces her to star Margo Channing and to Eve, Margo's nemesis, as a graduate of the "Copacabana School of Dramatic Arts," hardly an appropriate training ground for a serious actress. She says that DeWitt met her "in passing," unwittingly mocking herself, while Sanders arches his eyebrows and sighs condescendingly.

Miss Caswell's worst enemy is not the callous theatrical world, but herself. She insists on calling the butler a "waiter," because you just can't call out "'oh, butler', since someone's name may be Butler." A sneering Sanders tells her she has "a point, an idiotic point, but a point." Margo has the last word about Marilyn as she comforts the producer Max and treats his heartburn: "One good burp and you'll be rid of Miss Caswell."

Marilyn appears in *All About Eve* as a shiny young blonde, wearing a strapless gown and long hanging earrings. She is the ridiculous foil to Eve who cleverly remains closed about her ambitions until they can no longer be concealed. Sometimes Miss Caswell's obviousness is childlike. Sitting on

ALL ABOUT EVE (1950). As Miss Caswell

THE FIREBALL (1950). With Jim Brown and Mickey Rooney

HOMETOWN STORY (1951). With Alan Hale, Jr.

RIGHT CROSS (1950). With Dick Powell

the steps, she says, "There's something a girl could make sacrifices for. Sable!" When Max asks, "Did she say "sable" or "Gable?" she replies eagerly, "Either one."

The moment is autobiographical in several ways. It allows Marilyn to comment on her long-held crush on Clark Gable, and it reveals the depth of her ambition, something she has in common with Miss Caswell, although their means and aspirations differed.

In the part of Miss Caswell, most Hollywood producers convinced themselves that Marilyn was playing herself and that she too lacked talent and was utilizable only as a decorative blonde. It suited both their box-office needs and their view of women. Marilyn thus failed to land any serious parts for the next three years. On loan, she had bit roles in *The Fireball* (1950) with Mickey Rooney and in *Right Cross* (1950) with Dick Powell, where she again played the wrong kind of woman. In *Right Cross* she received no billing at all. She was also in a minor MGM film called *Hometown Story* (1951) as a secretary in a newspaper office.

Disliked by the studio bosses whom Marilyn aptly described later as "jealous of their power . . . like political bosses," she was dumped into a variety of Grade B films, the main effect and purpose of which was further to typecast her as the dumb blonde whose *raison d'etre* was to arouse the healthy impulses of every male around.

LOVE NEST (1951). With June Haver, William Lundigan, and Jack Paar

In *As Young As You Feel* (1951) Marilyn plays a secretary once again. Sexy and mediocre, if reasonably efficient, she is called "dear" by her boss, Mr. McKinley (Albert Dekker), whom she reminds to take his pills. When she speaks to customers, she affects a sexy voice, exactly as Marilyn the actress distinguished herself from Marilyn the woman.

She pours water for Mr. McKinley, who is duped in the film by star Monty Woolley, a factory worker masquerading as the company president in a campaign against a policy of forced retirement. Marilyn's dress is low-cut and her lines are invariably, "Yes, Mr. McKinley, Yes, Mr. McKinley." She takes minutes at company meetings, and knows every trivial fact asked by the boss, but she also wiggles from side to side as she walks, to his and others' delectation. The camera focuses on her plunging neckline. She wears a wristful of bangle bracelets and is properly awestruck and deferential to "big" men, as she tells Woolley, "I think your speech was grand. I felt honored to hear it." Decorative and looking slightly more like the future Marilyn, she is still allowed no means to develop a characterization with any range or subtlety.

Love Nest (1951), her next film, was no better. Marilyn played a former WAC comrade of hero William Lundigan, whose wife becomes jealous when Marilyn arrives to rent a room in their New York brownstone. Marilyn appears dressed up in high heels and veil, in marked contrast to frumpy June Haver who cleans the house and whines, "Couldn't we show our gratitude from a distance?"

The two women are set against each other—model Marilyn and housewife Haver. However hard she tries to be warm to Haver, her looks make it impossible for Marilyn to have a woman friend (as she would later comment about the absence of women friends in her own life). "Jim talked of nothing but you," says Monroe to Haver. "Jim can make anything interesting," is the wife's reply.

In *Let's Make It Legal* (1951) Marilyn plays Joyce, another blonde selling herself on the market in the hope of winning Zachary Scott's millions. It was a role she perfected demeaningly in *Gentlemen Prefer Blondes* two years later. Often the foil to the sweet girl next door (Haver in *Love Nest* or Jean Peters in *Niagara),* she was soon used by Hollywood to externalize the temptations to

AS YOUNG AS YOU FEEL (1951). With Albert Dekker

LET'S MAKE IT LEGAL (1951). With Macdonald Carey (to left of Marilyn)

which the flesh of men is heir.

In these films all good men shun her and she exists not as valuable in herself, but to justify by negative example the virtues of insipid, if less attractive upholders of the puritanical code Hollywood invoked to sanitize its exploitative depiction of sexual suggestion on the screen. What saved Monroe from a career of nothing but these roles was her gift for comedy and the sweet innocence with which she could not help but invest these *femmes fatales*.

This sweetness fully emerged in Marilyn's next film, *Clash By Night* (1952), made on loan to RKO Radio. In many ways interesting, *Clash By Night* is a second-rate morality play in which a woman (Barbara Stanwyck) spends years living her own life and returns home in defeat. She marries a doting if dull man (Paul Douglas), but her years of license make her prey to a predatory, exciting lover (Robert Ryan). Stanwyck knows she is "no good" and tries to pass on sound advice to young Peg (Marilyn) who, by showing signs of independence, risks Stanwyck's fate. The film's essential message is that women should remain in their places as loyal, dutiful wives if defiant folly is not to render them lonely, defeated, empty, and despised.

Clash By Night was directed by Fritz Lang and for once the role of dispenser of sex in the film belonged to the heroine, Barbara Stanwyck. This allowed Marilyn the rare opportunity to express other emotions, including compassion and good nature. Marilyn plays the girlfriend of Stanwyck's disapproving brother (Keith Andes), and through her character attempts to explore the choices open to a woman. She is a worker in a fish cannery who awakens in the morning with a loud yawn. She is then shown on the assembly line; her options are drudgery work or marriage. Emerging from the factory in dungarees, she eats a little chocolate to the objection of Joe (Andes), who disapproves because she'll "spread." Marilyn forcefully replies: "So, I'll spread . . . I suppose you'd beat me up too if I was your wife. I'd like to see you try, I'd like to see any man try . . . when I want any man to kiss me, I'll let you know by special messenger."

Marilyn is upset because a girl came to work with a black eye suffered in a beating by her husband; she is determined that no man will have her too easily. Although she is as sexy as the women she played in her earlier films, her character, uncommonly, has a measure of strength to which Marilyn proved

CLASH BY NIGHT (1952). As Peg

CLASH BY NIGHT (1952).
With Keith Andes

fully equal.

But Marilyn's words are destined to remain only rhetoric given the structure of society and woman's place, as perceived by the film. Stanwyck, who has returned home after ten years, finds few choices for a woman. Marilyn tries to resist, declaring at one point, "Who said I'd have kids?" But Joe quickly asserts his dominance: "You'd have kids!"

The film moralizes that Marilyn-Peg would be far better off to have children and remain "content" than become a woman like Mae (Stanwyck), alone in her late thirties, unsatisfied, and a prey to her own unsavory lusts. If young Peg, aged twenty, wants independence and her own life, Mae is there to tell her that "home is where you come when you run out of places." With such ideas of independence and self-sufficiency, Peg runs the risk of a fate like Mae's, for Mae at her age also had a desire for "her own life." Through Mae's sad trauma, Peg learns to accept the limited rewards that life offers. The film confirms Mae's advice to Peg to seek a man who can give her confidence, who can "take care of *her*."

Peg, like Mae, is aroused by Earl (Ryan): "He's kind of exciting," she remarks, thus establishing the supposed vulnerability of all women to a strong, silent, domineering man who shows her contempt. He calls Monroe "the honey, the fruit in the fruit tree." Peg giggles, naively innocent of her ability to attract men. She begins to sense this power which causes her to be reckless, intimating calamity if she is not tamed by marriage.

Peg finally becomes engaged to Joe, responding to the man who does not hesitate to slap or overpower a woman. She is important to the end of the film when she refuses to condemn Mae, because Mae's adulterous behavior forms a pattern to which all women are presumed vulnerable. Upon hearing that Mae is having an affair with Earl, she asks why Mae shouldn't enjoy herself. When Mae's affair with Earl becomes overt, Peg tells Joe, "You don't have the right to judge her."

The film itself is a paradigm of the typical movies of the fifties. Its bold subject of an independent woman who betrays a good man through adultery has the obligatory punishment of the partner who strays, especially if she is a woman. But Marilyn Monroe added a fresh, energetic dimension to *Clash By Night*. Her role, despite final capitulation to Joe, posed the idea that Mae's defiance and adultery had their origin in the latent desire of many working-class women to escape being tied to a lifetime of fathers, husbands, and demeaning drudgery. Their zest for life, if not

WE'RE NOT MARRIED (1952).
As Annabel Norris, "Mrs. Mississippi"

extinguished, escaped the confining limits of domesticity.

Unfortunately, once she returned to Twentieth Century-Fox, Marilyn was again confined to those mindless, stereotyped parts the studio was determined to impose upon her. In *We're Not Married* (1952), she is again cast as a body accompanied by an empty head. The film is about six couples who suddenly learn that the justice of the peace was unauthorized to perform their weddings and consequently that they're not legally married. Marilyn and David Wayne play one such couple.

Recalling those couples so deceived, Victor Moore, the justice of the peace who had begun the marrying before his license became valid, describes Marilyn as that "cute little girl ... wasn't she cute?" He describes her as having "blushed about everything." The director cuts to a Mrs. Mississippi beauty contest which Marilyn wins, while husband Wayne, in the audience with baby, looks on proudly. Marilyn receives her trophy and is giddy with delight. Her existence is defined by her physical beauty, and the high point of her life is when it is rewarded.

Wayne at home later at the stove, with the baby slamming his highchair for food, is less than enchanted by his wife's status as Mrs. Mississippi. When she finally arrives home, her manager is with her. They are about to attend an American Legion party in the hope that the Legion will send them to Atlantic City where Marilyn has a chance to become "Mrs. America." Wearing a crown, bathing suit, and an absurd little cape, Marilyn asks whether Mrs. Mississippi will really have a limousine? "How many rooms are there in the Mrs. Mississippi suite?" she asks.

Husband Wayne remains home with baby until the mailman brings the news that they're not married. Wayne is delighted. "If there are any more diapers to be hung out," he asserts, "she's gonna hang 'em." Marilyn reads the letter and stares blankly, finally screeching, "You mean it means we're not married any more?" She throws her arms around him, crying, "How wonderful!"

If she seems stupid, she is also single-minded. The next cut is to the *Miss* Mississippi contest with Marilyn parading down the runway as the winner, blowing kisses to Wayne and baby. What carries the sequence is the spirit, energy, and radiance of Monroe as Miss Mississippi. If she is dumb, she also understands her own value and cleverly pursues her chance. The film itself, despite some amusing moments, is sheer pablum.

Don't Bother To Knock (1952) at

WE'RE NOT MARRIED (1952). With David Wayne and James Gleason

DON'T BOTHER TO KNOCK (1952). With director Roy Baker

least provided Marilyn with her first dramatic starring role. Unfortunately, the film itself was so ill-conceived and poorly written it could only serve her badly by suggesting to critics she was at fault for the film's failure. Bosley Crowther in *The New York Times* presented the predetermined view consistent with Hollywood's image of her: "All the equipment that Miss Monroe has to handle the job are a childishly blank expression and a provokingly feeble voice."

The fault was not hers at all. Marilyn was cast as a psychotic baby-sitter, working class in origin, but the film provided only the vaguest indication of the origin of her mental imbalance. It offers no coherent account of the weakness in her personality which made her vulnerable to insanity. We learn only that she became unbalanced when her fiance was killed in the Second World War.

Marilyn is indeed vacant and "not there" in this film, but her interpretation of the dissociated baby-sitter could not draw on any preceding development of character. She likes being in the hotel where the baby-sitting assignment takes place, and her early friendli-

DON'T BOTHER TO KNOCK (1952). With Richard Widmark

MONKEY BUSINESS (1952). As Lois Laurel

MONKEY BUSINESS (1952). With Cary Grant and Charles Coburn

ness toward the child and her parents is convincing. To the child she promises to make up a story and to the parents she wishes "a beautiful evening."

She seems obsequious and correct, if not terribly interested in the child. The first hint we have of the sitter's derangement occurs when she tells the parents she never eats candy and then proceeds to stuff herself with it as soon as they leave. Nor is she willing to read the child a second story. But these are hardly the acts of a psychotic character. They are too trivial and ordinary. Only the blank expression on Marilyn's face is available to her to convey that she is more a part of another delusionary world than of this one.

It is perhaps a tribute to her acting that when Marilyn tries on the jewelry and evening dress of Mrs. Jones, she avoids appearing any more attractive than she had in her own shabby dress. She manages to attract the attention of a man whose room is across the alley, played by Richard Widmark. He tells her she "sounds peculiar" when they speak on the telephone. A telling moment in the film occurs when she signals to Widmark to come over. As she sits down at the dressing table, a tilt of the camera down to a close-up reveals the deep scars on her wrists. Her look of horror when she learns that Widmark is a pilot is also powerful. She asks if he flew a bomber during the war and becomes quite agitated, confusing

O'HENRY'S FULL HOUSE (1952). With Charles Laughton

him with her dead lover: "You were rescued. You came back." She kisses him on the mouth not out of present lust, but in memory of a lost love. The dreamy quality of Marilyn's performance is right—the correlative demeanor for the particular psychosis she bears, her need to live in the past because she cannot accept a loss so great that to feel it fully would destroy her.

There is enough information in the film to suggest at least the roots of the girl's dissatisfaction with her life. "All through high school," she says, "I never had a dress to wear at night." Her parents beat her if she showed liking for a boy. But these glimpses are not developed. In the girl's confusion when the child wakes up and disturbs her liaison with Widmark, whom she by now completely identifies with her dead lover, she almost commits murder. Yet she manages at her best moments in the film to convey pathos: "If you just let someone walk away from you," she says, "you'll never find anyone to take their place." The line could be one out of the life of Norma Jean Baker.

At the end, through compassion for this sick girl, Widmark is able to find in himself an "understanding heart," the lack of which had destroyed his relationship with his alienated girlfriend, Anne Bancroft. Marilyn crawls out the hotel-

NIAGARA (1953).
With Richard Allan

NIAGARA (1953). As Rose Loomis

room door breathing heavily. There is a fine shot of her standing behind the bars of the elevator as she waits for them to open, even as she is locked behind the bars of her own past and her thwarted love for the pilot killed in the Pacific. Her parting words as she is taken away by a policeman are about people who love each other. She makes quite convincing her pained recognition that Widmark is not her former lover: "They told me you were buried in the sea. I don't want to harm anybody." If there is little range in the characterization, it is not because of Marilyn Monroe's contribution, but because of the inadequacy of a tired and pitifully melodramatic script, lacking, among other things, even the suspense essential to melodrama.

Seizing on the poor reviews, Fox refused to cast Marilyn in another serious dramatic role. *Don t Bother To Knock* was followed by *Monkey Business* (1952), a vehicle for the comic antics of Cary Grant and

Ginger Rogers, who take a youth serum returning them to adolescence and childhood. Marilyn plays Lois Laurel, the secretary of Grant's boss, Charles Coburn, who is asked why he has a stenographer who can't type, take dictation or spell. Marilyn walks past and Coburn luridly gets the "comic" line at her expense: "Well, *any* stenographer can spell!"

Marilyn is even dumber than usual. She tells Grant that her boss had been complaining about her "punctuation," so she arrived at work earlier. After he swallows the youth serum, Grant engages in a series of escapades with Marilyn, taking her driving at high speeds. She asks him if his motor is running and he retorts: "Is yours?" Her giggling is infectious if half-idiotic as they speed along. Again Marilyn is the sex object and the literal butt of most of the jokes. When Coburn and his board of directors take the serum, Coburn proceeds to squirt seltzer water at Monroe.

An ordinary Hollywood comedy, the film is instructive regarding Marilyn Monroe. She is featured yet again as a mindless body capable of being cast only as the unfeeling receptacle of the desires and abuse of others. The longer Twentieth Century-Fox persisted in casting Marilyn Monroe in such parts, the harder it became for her to dissociate the screen persona from her real self.

In *O. Henry's Full House* (1952), Marilyn played a whore in a very brief role opposite Charles Laughton. Wishing to commit a minor crime which would land him in a warm jail for the winter, vagrant Laughton backs off when he realizes that she is a streetwalker. Marilyn is fetching in a muff and black cape. When Laughton apologizes for his mistake, she becomes angry in an effective street accent: "Hey, what is this? You trying to kid me?" Laughton gallantly offers her his cane as a souvenir, but the moment makes a deep impression on the girl, who murmurs incredulously, "He called me a lady," and she breaks into sobs. In this very small part Marilyn is moving, with a helplessness and innocence she had the opportunity to project fully only much later in her last complete film, *The Misfits*.

Niagara (1953) finally made Marilyn a star. After it was released, Monroe moved to star row at Fox. In this film she performed one of the first of her nude scenes, behind a curtain in the shower, and she was billed over Joseph Cotten, her co-star. Still the role offered Marilyn no greater range than had *Don't Bother To Knock*. It was the only film in which she was maliciously and absolutely evil without her usual redeeming graces of innocence and naïveté.

Rose Loomis (Monroe) plots with her lover to kill her husband George (Cotten). George kills Rose's lover instead, and in his semi-dementia he goes on to kill his wife. Cotten is suffering from an old war wound, which brings on jealous rages. His sensual wife craves passion and excitement and has neither sympathy nor concern for her husband's struggle to find a cure for his depression. Monroe is the stereotype of the lustful, manipulative and selfish woman. The opening shot finds her in bed with a cigarette, pretending to be asleep when her husband enters the room and calls to her. Like the color of the dress she wears in a crucial sequence, she is a "scarlet" woman. She wears blood-red lipstick to bed and true to the stereotype, her bathrobe is trimmed with fur.

The wide-eyed concern she affects when relating her husband's trauma to others is quickly replaced by cynical rudeness when she is alone with Cotten inside their cabin. Her daytime suit is skin tight, as is her evening dress when she walks off to meet her lover, her hips swinging in brazen

NIAGARA (1953). With Joseph Cotten

undulation. The film made the Monroe walk famous. Rose sways along on her way to plot the murder which will free her fróm a sick, dependent husband.

Rose does display some of the characteristic Monroe zest and eagerness, but this is held to a minimum in keeping with her image as a murderess whom the audience muust condemn. She is anxious to hear "the laughter of kids" and to have good times. In her tight shower cap, she embodies energy waiting to burst free, unnaturally and unjustly contained. She plays the song "Kiss" repeatedly on the record player and sways and hums along. Her eyes are dreamy, her lips are parted, and the sensuous mouth is accentuated by dangling, looped earrings.

She exists as an entity unto herself as the words of the song assert a torrid state of being: "Take me, take me in your arms ... darling, don't forsake me, kiss me, hold me tight." The "Kiss" sequence is abruptly interrupted by Cotten who breaks the record in fury, partly to prevent this amoral, but magnetically sensuous, Marilyn from remaining on screen too long. Otherwise, her subsequent murder would become less acceptable, despite the intended poetic justice.

The combined emotion of desire and resentment Cotten feels for the wife he calls a "tramp" gets "out of hand—like those Falls." Niagara Falls provides a correlative of the passion of Rose for her lover, but also of Loomis for the Rose he picked up in a beer hall. The second half of the film belongs to Cotten. Rose's behavior becomes demonic as she laughs uncontrollably after she and Cotten make love on the night before she is to have him murdered. She is vicious when he becomes jealous at the prospect of her going off alone to buy bus tickets. She now taunts her husband, denying while simultaneously implying her imminent rendezvous, with the words "anybody suits me."

Marilyn's acting occasionally becomes forced, as when she reads the "t" in "about" in too pronounced a manner. She is best when, free of the film's inane dialogue, she can be herself. One of her finer moments occurs with her walk along the river. She smiles with teeth showing as her tryst song is played on the bell tower, a prearranged signal that their plans are proceeding without obstacle.

Another good scene occurs in a hospital to which Rose has been taken. She has learned that it was her lover and not her husband who was pushed over the falls. Having fainted, she is shown in bed writhing in semi-consciousness. The scene's power is again helped by the absence of flat dialogue. Rose,

GENTLEMEN PREFER BLONDES (1953). With Jane Russell

GENTLEMEN PREFER BLONDES (1953). With Jane Russell

now wild with fright, wakes up despite the heavy sedation. She escapes from the hospital, but is pursued by Loomis to the top of the bell tower.

She runs frantically with hair flying in disarray as her husband's steps are heard gaining on her. The strangulation is shot in an arty, if unusual, montage sequence, the sole relief from otherwise uninventive photography. Loomis strangles Rose, while a series of short shots of the bells from different angles are arranged before us in close-up. On the eighth shot of the bells, Loomis releases her neck and she falls. There are two views of her dead body: one in long focus, the other a middle shot. She lies in a patch of light surrounded by darkness, again rather heavily symbolizing the balance of qualities in her nature. The light suggests her energy and vitality and the darkness her cruel amorality.

But the role utterly limited rather than expanded the horizon of Marilyn's screen persona. The film shows not the slightest concern for, or even the necessity of exploring, what made her the way she is. It did not allow her one line of dialogue which would explain or justify her, creating some minimal measure of ambiguity in an utterly

HOW TO MARRY A MILLIONAIRE (1953). As Pola

one-sided character. The conception of Rose sums up not only the industry's view of Marilyn, but also its predominant image of women. They are either loyal wives, as personified by the good-hearted woman (Jean Peters) who tries to help George Loomis, or they are whores whose fate is delayed long enough for their sexuality to be enjoyed.

Niagara was followed by two similar films, *Gentlemen Prefer Blondes* (1953) and *How To Marry A Millionaire* (1953). In both, Monroe plays a mindless blonde out to snare a rich husband. Both films are heavy-handed, drumming in the theme that this is the *raison d'etre* of every attractive woman if she is normal and true to instinct. In *Gentlemen Prefer Blondes*, Monroe manages to land her millionaire; in the second film she settles for a theoretically rich man played by David Wayne, who will become solvent, hopefully, once he clears up a "mistake" with Internal Revenue.

In *Gentlemen Prefer Blondes* Loreli (Marilyn) is described as a woman who "can stand on the stage with a spotlight in her eyes and still see a diamond in a man's pocket," the ironic opposite of Pola in *How to Marry A Millionaire* who is "blind as a bat," yet refuses to wear glasses because an eligible rich man would not desire her. Loreli will do anything to trap her man. She even tells her prospective father-in-law: "I don't want to marry your son for his money. I want to marry him for *your* money." The theme of the film is expressed by Monroe at its conclusion: "A man being rich is like a girl being pretty." The force of this argument is so devastating it changes the mind of her recalcitrant would-be father-in-law.

You wouldn't want your daughter to marry a poor man, Loreli reasons. So why would you want your son to marry a woman who didn't desire a rich husband? The exchange is interesting because it unwittingly touches on the double standard wherein the obsession with money is unscrupulous in the poor, but not in the rich. The rich may justifiably scorn those without money, but the poor may not. And the rich man's father has to admit that a gold-digging woman is only the other side of the coin of his own insistence on a moneyed wife for his son.

Loreli epitomizes the woman who has only her body and her submissiveness to barter. Her dress is slit way up the side. She is constantly thrusting herself forward to expose her breasts. Complementing her total definition of herself in terms of the physical is a crassness at once too vulgar and far too serious to be funny. She will asso-

HOW TO MARRY A MILLIONAIRE (1953). With Betty Grable

HOW TO MARRY A MILLIONAIRE (1953). With Betty Grable and Lauren Bacall

ciate with a man only if he's a millionaire, and the point of this outrageous film is that while Loreli may *appear* stupid (she voyages to Europe, France) she is really clever because she knows how to trap a rich man. The intelligent Dorothy (Jane Russell) is really foolish because *she* marries for love.

Viewing this film twenty years after it was made, the spectacle of a woman being made the butt of humor for trying to put a tiara she covets around her neck is not funny. It is a tribute to Marilyn Monroe that she was perceptive enough to be revolted by roles like that of Loreli Lee. Marilyn must have winced at having to say, "I can be smart when it's important, but most men don't like it."

In *How To Marry A Millionaire* Marilyn is believable as Pola who is always walking into doors because she will never wear her glasses in the presence of a man. Her generosity leads her to invite her friend Loco (Betty Grable) to share the apartment with her and her roommate, Schatze (Lauren Bacall). It also accounts for her choice of

Wayne, a man whose prospects are by no means certain, despite her purpose of scheming to entrap a millionaire.

Yet her near-sightedness in the film is characterized as stupidity. She sits in an airplane intently reading a book upside down. She then discovers she has taken the wrong plane and is going to *Kansas* and not *Atlantic* City. She lusts for a Rockefeller and when asked which one, she replies, "I don't care."

Throughout the film, Monroe, Grable and Bacall regale each other with fantasies of wealth. They have rented a lavish furnished apartment in order to meet millionaires, and they sell off its furniture to pay the rent. Marilyn's dream is to find a man who will load her arms with invaluable gems. Hollywood, of course, tries to have it all ways. Each of the three women finally marries a man she loves and only one turns out to be a genuine millionaire.

Marilyn's basic gag—that of bumping into waiters, the walls or, in one scene, steps—while she models a stunning red bathing suit—is carried off well. And as an actress, Marilyn holds her own with Grable and Bacall, although the real achievement for all three is to finish the film without falling asleep.

Marilyn spent six hours and twenty minutes being made up and dressed for the premiere of this film and was greeted as a star at last. On her way home, she made a stop at Fox to return her dress and accessories. That such a role and characterization should be a turning point in her career best explains the futility and tragedy of her effort to be treated by Hollywood and its public-relations machine as a serious actress and an intelligent human being.

Sandwiched between the light-headed *How To Marry A Millionaire* and an inane musical vehicle for Ethel Merman, *There's No Business Like Show Business*, Monroe starred in a western called *River Of No Return* (1954), which she considered with justification the worst film of her career. Marilyn plays a lady of easy virtue, a singer in a mining-town saloon in love with a selfish gambler played by Rory Calhoun, and later with a farmer played by Robert Mitchum. When Calhoun leaves her to file a mining claim, Monroe and Mitchum follow him down the tumultuous river of the film's title.

At the beginning of the film, Marilyn makes her entrance in the red-sequin corset and black-net stockings which have become obligatory in every Grade B western featuring a saloon singer. She sings "One Silver Dollar," celebrating the values of this corrupt

RIVER OF NO RETURN (1954). As Kay

RIVER OF NO RETURN (1954), With Robert Mitchum and Tommy Rettig

"Sodom and Gomorrah," and is little better than the gambler who will abandon her.

But she's also the whore with a heart of gold who befriends Mitchum's lost young son, Mark. The child calls her "a lady," providing respect for which she hungers. At the beginning of the film, Marilyn is shown polishing the red shoes that are her trademark; in the end, having yielded to the kindness of her own nature, aided by the presence of the child, she flings the shoes away and is ready to become a good woman as Mitchum's wife.

Men drool as she waves the train of her costume in their faces, but the film, having established that she's physically arousing, now prepares for her rescue by a strong man. She helps Mitchum and the boy recover and escape from the Indians and so earns a better fate than that of saloon hostess. This is heralded by the innocent song she sings to the boy throughout the film—a song about the harmony of nature and one completely inappropriate to her kind of woman: "Old Father Christmas/Trims all the trees/Down in the meadow/Snow softly clings. . . ."

Yet like all the roles Marilyn played in the course of her career, Kay is provided no insight into her own character. It is true that she cites her poverty and that of Calhoun to explain why they scheme to escape it, but events in general are invariably beyond her control. She is ruled by instinct. The film begins by criticizing women whose beauty, says Mitchum, is "only skin deep," but it ends by making Kay the ideal woman because she finally submits to the strong silent Mitchum, the counterpart male image sold by Hollywood.

At the beginning of the film Kay longs for fancy gowns, to live in "swell hotels" and to go to the opera. The film condemns not her dreams of comfort, but her independence, for she imagines herself self-sufficient and able to command respect—which "opera goers," as opposed to saloon singers, automatically receive. She wants to reach above herself, and although this is approved for men like Mitchum, Kay must be punished for such presumption. Respectability means placing her sexual skills at the service of one man and accepting him as arbiter and master of her fate. At the end, with no enlargement of her understanding, she is ready to return to the wilds with Mitchum and the boy to become a housewife.

Marilyn's acting in this film is unconvincing. Under the guidance of Natasha Lytess, she was taught a form of enunciation unsuitable either to her own personality or to the character she played. When she says "The whole country's crawling with Indians and you're going fishing?", the line is read as if out of a high-school play. Her performance is effective only when she talks to the boy, well acted by Tommy Rettig. Her lines to Mitchum, "You couldn't understand. He didn't treat me like a tramp. He treated me like a woman," make one wince.

As in *Niagara*, Marilyn's best moments occur when she does not have to speak. She is persuasive, for example, in the scene in which she is ill. Shivering with cold and soaked by fevered perspiration, her hair is unkempt and she is without make-up. Mitchum massages her to keep her from freezing, and her demeanor is persuasive. It is instructive that in the brief moments when Marilyn Monroe looks like an actual person instead of a dolled-up manikin, her ability to act emerges.

As in virtually all Monroe's films, the lack of credibility is due fundamentally to the script rather than to anyone's performance. At the film's conclusion, she is literally carried off over Mitchum's shoulder. He has not bothered to ascertain her willingness, and she responds automatically to his imposition of will à la Hollywood caveman. "Real" men use physical prowess to tame recalcitrant

THERE'S NO BUSINESS LIKE SHOW BUSINESS (1954). With Donald O'Connor

women and women secretly crave to be so enslaved by men who will do all the thinking and deciding. The last shot of the film is of her red shoes lying in the dust as their wagon moves off.

Marilyn's psychological equilibrium could not bear the imprint of the roles in which she was cast. Inwardly she must have feared they expressed the director's true estimate of her character and that he saw through the superficial façade provided by "Marilyn" which could not successfully conceal the inadequacies of Norma Jean.

In *There's No Business Like Show Business* (1954), a film which Monroe never wanted to do, she played a hatcheck girl named Vicky. Although for Marilyn it was no proud accomplishment, she shocked the Hollywood of the fifties with a number called "Heat Wave." It was shot through a red filter with Marilyn dressed up as a blonde Carmen Miranda flirtatiously calling the male dancers "honey" in the manner of Mae West. In the close-ups her lips cover her gums as she was taught. Marilyn, through lack of real alternatives, had slipped once more into the role of sexpot.

Show Business is in reality a non-film. It has virtually no plot, merely one production number after another strung together. Marilyn is a hat-check girl "temporarily between (singing) assignments." Her hair is made up like cotton candy, and the film constantly jokes belittlingly about her acting aspirations.

Donald O'Connor laughs at the idea of her playing Lady Macbeth. Marilyn in the film even tries to convince a producer that "she's an actress, too." Such autobiographical touches do little to make the character of Vicky convincing as an ambitious nightclub singer.

Monroe's best numbers are "After You Get What You Want, You Don't Want It" (which could stand as an epigram for her life) and "Heat Wave." The former has her dressed in a white-lace see-through costume, her breasts thrust forward. The little hat-check girl of a moment before has become a torrid dancer on display to avid men. The song itself strongly conveys Marilyn's own plight, arriving at a stardom that "Vicky" and Norma Jean envied, but at a dismal cost to her self.

THERE'S NO BUSINESS LIKE SHOW BUSINESS (1954)
With Ethel Merman, Dan Dailey, Mitzi Gaynor, and Donald O'Connor

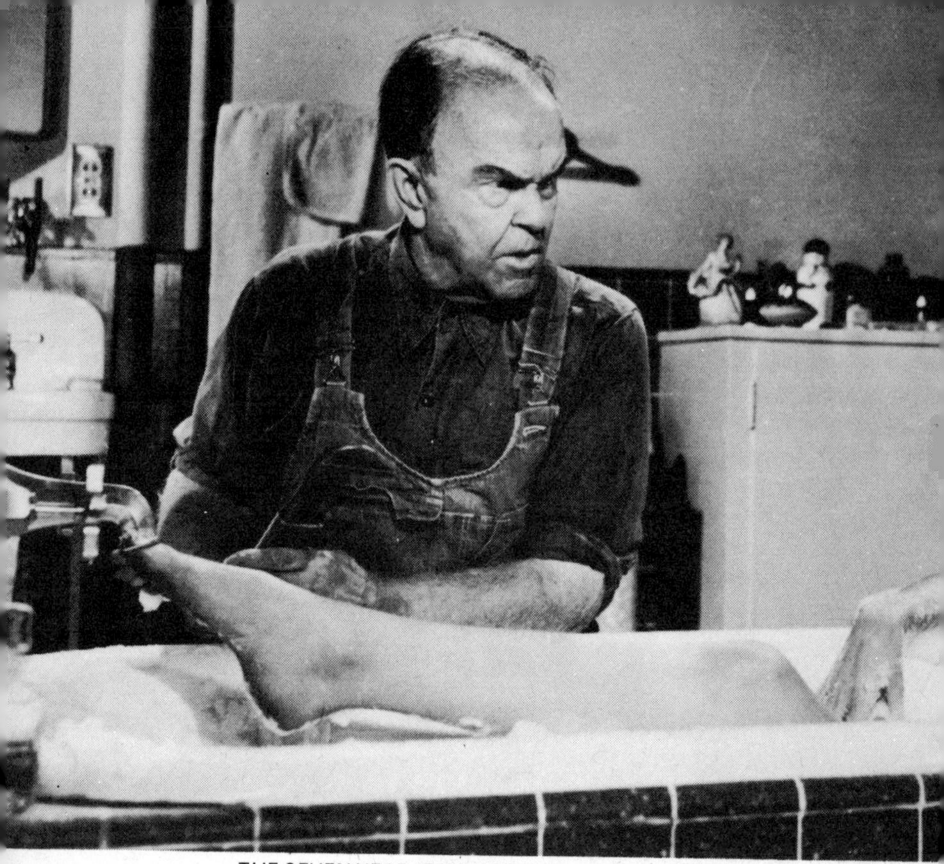

THE SEVEN YEAR ITCH (1955). With Victor Moore

Like the real Marilyn, Vicky is transformed once she achieves this success. She is given a new name and new clothes. Her manager begins "doing her over completely." The "Heat Wave" number reveals a totally new Vicky, as if she is transformed into Marilyn herself. Her shyness is replaced by a siren who flaunts her breasts as she leans over to read the weather report in the newspaper. Simultaneously, she throws herself into as many bumps and grinds as she can manage amid filters, smoke, and rolling drums. Vicky and Norma Jean are now successful stars. They are also condemned forever to bump and grind for an audience which enjoys their enslavement and defines them by it.

This film, like its predecessors, could do nothing for Marilyn. Her singing was adequate, but the character she played had so little depth and nuance that her dramatic abil-

ity could neither appear nor develop. Her last film under the old contract with Fox was *The Seven Year Itch* (1955). Relentlessly, it cast her again as a dumb blonde, allowing her, however, to show some measure of comic talent. As "The Girl" living upstairs from Tom Ewell, she becomes the object of his sexual fantasies, as Marilyn herself became for millions of men.

Like every film in which Marilyn would appear until her death, the center of the story involves the male character and his conflicts. Her basic purpose is to be his foil. Never having a role as a woman capable of intellectual inquiry, she could never experience in her parts either conflicts of consciousness, problems of decision-making, or dilemmas of moral choice. In all her films without exception, she is amoral, like "The Girl" upstairs, willing to have an affair with Ewell if he wishes. She exists in a realm of the physical beyond moral sensitivity. "The Girl" prefers married men because "it can't get drastic." This is good since men are forever falling in love with her. She objects to marriage in a nutty, common-sensical way because "that would be worse than living at the club. I'd have to start getting in at one again."

"The Girl," in fact, is more a fantasy of Sherman, the semi-pornographic publisher, than she is a real person. We first meet her in tight skirt and white spiked heels. The voice is even more whispery than Marilyn's had been to date as she juts out her buttocks simpering, "my fan's caught in the door." It is difficult to believe that she is a real person.

The crash of the tomato plant she drops from her balcony on the beachchair Sherman had just vacated best expresses the lack of

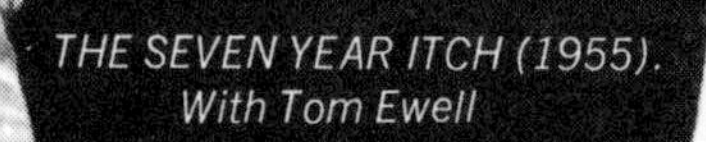

THE SEVEN YEAR ITCH (1955).
With Tom Ewell

THE SEVEN YEAR ITCH. With Tom Ewell, Robert Strauss, and Sonny Tufts

subtlety characterizing "The Girl." She was naked while on the balcony because "my underwear is in the icebox." It is not only the New York summer, presumably, which requires her to keep her sizzling pants in the freezer! Sherman immediately falls into the fantasy in which "The Girl," wearing a slinky strapless gown and long black gloves, leans over the piano as he plays Rachmaninoff. Her enraptured lines are: "It shakes me, it quakes me, it makes me feel goose-pimply all over."

We learn little in the course of the film about "The Girl." She does television commercials, but where she came from or what other relationships she has in her life we do not discover. She is never given a name, let alone an identity, and she refers to herself without a qualm as "the tomato from upstairs," who like a potted plant drops into Sherman's life.

Part of the comic talent Marilyn invests in the character stems from the hapless nature of "The Girl." She sleeps in the bathtub to cool off and puts her big toe in the dripping faucet so that it won't keep her awake. Her toe becomes stuck and she has to call the plumber (Victor Moore) to rescue her. The role conceives of "The Girl" as less bright than a chimpanzee and at least as mischievous.

Worse, the characterization makes thinly veiled allusions to Monroe herself. Like the real Marilyn, "The Girl" once posed for an "artistic picture," a barely concealed reference to the famous calendar. Now she appears on the "Dazzle-Dent Toothpaste Hour," suggestive of and in no way inferior to roles the real Marilyn had been given from *How To Marry A Millionaire* to *There's No Business Like Show Business*. "The Girl" admires the drama and wishes she had seen Sarah Bernhardt, again a direct suggestion of Monroe herself, and the fact that "The Girl" is cretinous is scarcely unintended. Hence not

BUS STOP (1956). With Don Murray, Hope Lange, and Betty Field

only does the part fix Monroe in a demeaning role, but she is made to ridicule herself as well. Like the real Marilyn, "The Girl" is lonely. She has bought champagne to drink alone on her twenty-second birthday, but, predictably, she has been unable to open the bottle.

If "The Girl" is presented as an object, a male sexual fantasy come alive, she is only an *unconscious* flirt. She tells Sherman he has "powerful thumbs," evidently oblivious of her suggestiveness. Everything said or heard she construes literally, befitting her utter lack of acquaintance with things of the mind. The double entendre is presented as beyond her meager grasp. Ewell evokes what is intended to represent the typical American male, aroused only by women without intellect or a center of gravity. He couldn't care less whether she is an Eddie Fisher fan or prefers fish and chips, as long as she is deferential, available and arousing.

This matter-of-factness is necessary to the film. "The Girl's" lack of concern about the attitude of men to her as a person softens completely the moral question of implied adultery. This facilitates the requisite ending in which Sherman goes off in quest of his wife and son, nothing having "happened" between himself and "The Girl."

For "The Girl" has been no more than a child. She stands at the top of the street-level subway grating because the hot stream of air when a train passes feels good as it flows up her legs. Her pleated skirt repeatedly blows up to her waist, but despite Joe DiMaggio's discomfort on the set, the moment is utterly innocent, really the action of a small child. "Ohhh . . . here comes another one," she squeals. Sherman "tricks" her into kissing him to test the truth of the Dazzle Dent commercial. The act is equally innocuous and devoid of lust. Her real motive in wishing to spend the night in Sherman's apartment is to gain the benefit of the air conditioner. He sleeps on the living-room couch. It is in equally childish innocence that she descends the interior stairs to Sherman's apartment, having come through the trap door: "You know what? We can do this all summer."

Through the force of her personality, Marilyn manages sufficiently to overcome the part, to grant "The Girl" not only childlike sexiness, but real kindness. She is kind to Sherman in the same manner as she feels sorry at the end for *The Creature From The Black Lagoon*, a movie they see together: "He wasn't all bad. He just craved a little affection." She salves Sherman's ego, assuring him that not every girl wants a man who looks like

BUS STOP (1956). On the set

Gregory Peck: "You think every girl's a dope?" She describes men who are not noticed at first: "Way over in the corner . . . you sense he's gentle and kind . . . that's what's really exciting." And she flatters Sherman: "If I were your wife, I'd be very jealous of you. I'd be very, very jealous. I think you're just elegant."

Monroe's inflection when she recites the word "elegant" grants a moment of dignity and character to "The Girl." It briefly lifts her beyond the image of childlike sex queen. It displays the individuality, poise and grace of which the actress Marilyn Monroe was capable, given a modicum of opportunity.

Nothing in the remainder of the film can approximate this moment. Sherman informs a friend who drops in that the blonde in the kitchen is "Marilyn Monroe," again making explicit the attempt to

BUS STOP (1956). With Don Murray

equate the conception of "The Girl" with the woman Monroe. At the end "The Girl" encourages Sherman to induce his wife to appreciate him more by letting him know that other women find him attractive, a note of kindness which again allows Monroe some scope in the characterization.

She kisses him good-bye, urging him not to wipe the lipstick off his face: "If your wife thinks it's cranberry juice, tell her she's got cherry pits in her head." She tosses his shoes out the window to him, and with a wave and flourish the film ends. The moments of *joie de vivre* with which Marilyn Monroe manages to endow her portrayal of "The Girl" finally illuminate a film which, despite such minor concessions, is fundamentally an overelaborated and tiresome gag at "The Girl's" expense. With a character more a fantasy than a real woman, Marilyn accomplished a minor miracle, adding small notes of individuality to give "The Girl" life. Her presence transforms the film.

After *The Seven Year Itch* Marilyn said good-bye to Hollywood and established a permanent residence in New York. The first film with her new production company was *Bus Stop* (1956). Her performance was considered by many to be the finest of her career.

Hollywood met a new Marilyn with *Bus Stop*. She rejected frilly costumes and searched Fox's wardrobe department for the darned stockings and seedy lamé coat with monkey-fur she wears in the film. In one love scene she plays with Don Murray, a string of saliva was momentarily visible as their lips parted. She protested furiously when the moment was cut from the film. Monroe sought authenticity and constantly tried to lend seriousness and conviction to an essentially weak and superficial script. The white make-up Cherie wears was Marilyn's idea.

Now Marilyn was also ruthless about her own image. She insisted that Hope Lange's hair be darkened because it looked too much like her own. When director Joshua Logan refused, Marilyn stalked off the set and waited him out. Although a small matter, its importance to her reflected years of being pushed around, ill-used and imposed upon.

As Cherie, Marilyn, more than in any of her films, played herself. Coinciding with her heavy drinking and pill-taking, was the increasing merger of Marilyn's screen character with facets of her real self. *Bus Stop* is partly about Cherie, a saloon singer who can't sing, as many said that Marilyn couldn't act.

She avoids the men she is hired to entertain, uncomfortable with

THE PRINCE AND THE SHOWGIRL (1957). With Laurence Olivier

having to flaunt herself before them, even as Marilyn was at heart. "I've been tryin' to be somebody," Cherie says, "like Hildegarde [a well-known *chanteuse*, as Cherie calls herself a chantoose]. Can you imagine her sitting down between her numbers on some truck driver's lap?" She yearns, like Marilyn, to be taken seriously in her profession. She imagines, as had Norma Jean, that she will find this at Hollywood and Vine: "You get discovered, tested, options—you get treated with a little respect, too." Her hillbilly accent is exact and her longings recognizable, an explicit echo of Marilyn's own.

Cherie is a girl innocent of her sexuality, who doesn't know what to say to men. She lacks confidence and must be supplied with inane jokes by a waitress friend (Eileen Heckart) in order to overcome her shyness in conversation. Her num-

THE PRINCE AND THE SHOWGIRL (1957). With Sybil Thorndike and Richard Wattis

THE PRINCE AND THE SHOWGIRL (1957). With Laurence Olivier

ber, "That Old Black Magic," is performed so ineptly, with stumbling and scared voice, that it is moving. She twists her head awkwardly. Her black-satin gloves slip precariously down her arms as she aimlessly waves a frowsy blue scarf. Shabby black net covers her breasts. She is languid, thin, weak and pallid.

But Bo (Don Murray), a young rancher down for the rodeo, sees her as his "angel, so pale and white" and is determined to marry her. He silences the crowd of noisy, jeering cowboys and at the conclusion of her number, he proposes. Cherie likes him because "you made them have respect too. I like that... When I realized you was doing it for me, I was attracted to you." But she soon learns he is an adolescent bully, treating her like a purchased steer or the heifer he ropes. At one point he even lassoes her with the same rope. She rejects him.

At the film's end, when he receives his symbolic comeuppance in the form of a beating at the hands of the bus conductor, he apologizes and treats her like a woman with her own mind who is far more experienced than he. Interestingly, it is only when he receives a humiliating beating, and apologizes to all, that she can respect him as a man and not reject him as an obnoxious boy. The film, rare in this respect for Hollywood, explicitly inverts and ridicules the *machismo* worship associating brutality with maleness.

The scene in which Bo barges into her bedroom is well played. Waking Cherie after she has had only three hours sleep, he is anxious to get her out into the fresh air: "No wonder you're so pale and white." She covers her face with a pillow. Her bedsheets are gray and crumpled. She says she hates parades, but he drags her out against her will.

Like all the characters Marilyn would play, Cherie is dim-witted. She signs the marriage license because "I had to do something.

THE PRINCE AND THE SHOWGIRL (1957). As Elsie Marina

SOME LIKE IT HOT (1959). As Sugar Kane

SOME LIKE IT HOT (1959). With Tony Curtis and Jack Lemmon (left)

He was making such a fuss in front of all those people." She looks at her forty-three-dollar engagement ring and says, "It ain't exactly a diamond and it ain't exactly not a diamond, either." When she bends over to put on her lipstick, two leering photographers take a picture of her rear end. Like Marilyn, despite her craving for acceptance and respect, people are interested only in her body.

Cherie even misses a cue a child could manage. Instead of using the planned pretext of leaving to "powder her nose" so she can escape from Bo, she takes out her compact where she is and announces she will literally powder her nose. She is, in fact, the very "poor helpless little animal" she accuses Bo of pushing around in the rodeo. When Bo pulls part of her costume off, she can only scream fatuously, "I hate you and I despise you. Give me back my tail." The joke, as usual, is on and not with her.

Lassoed and virtually kidnapped onto the bus bound for Bo's ranch, Cherie confides her hopes to Elma (Hope Lange). She wonders "if there's the kind of love I have in mind," a plaintive cry uttered so often by Marilyn Monroe. Cherie was "almost married" to a cousin at fourteen, just as Marilyn herself was married at sixteen. Cherie wants "a guy I can look up to and admire, but I don't want him to browbeat me." She longs for someone with "some real regard for me aside from all that loving stuff," even as Marilyn wished to be admired for something other than her body.

This conversation with Elma meant a great deal to Marilyn Monroe. She was constantly breaking off, unable to continue. Director Logan was never able to complete a full take. In desperation, he had to piece the scene together, and there is a telltale hint of this cut-and-paste job in one pointless cutaway to Bo and his friend Virge sitting in the back of the bus. (It took Marilyn eleven days to film the six-minute sequence of "My Heart Belongs To Daddy" in *Let's Make Love* because that number, too, evoked so much intense and disorienting personal feeling).

After lifting Cherie over his shoulder, Bo attempts brutishly to carry her off to a preacher while smacking her rump as she screams. Once he is set straight and apologizes, Cherie admits, "I ain't the kind of gal you thought I was... I had a real wicked life." She maintains he is better off without her,

SOME LIKE IT HOT (1959). With Tony Curtis

SOME LIKE IT HOT (1959). Sugar cuts the ice.

SL(20

but, to Bo's credit, he doesn't agree. At this, Cherie tells him, "I'd go anywhere in the world with you now." She throws away the map on which she had plotted her intended progress to Hollywood and Vine, and the film ends happily. "Ain't it wonderful when someone so terrible turns out to be so nice," says the intuitive Cherie. It is a feeling performance for Marilyn, confirming her ability at least to play a role that reflected her own life.

The Prince And The Showgirl (1957) was her next film, an uninspired attempt at sophisticated comedy directed by Laurence Olivier, who made the mistake of starring in the film as well. Monroe is a showgirl named Elsie Marina, who, like Marilyn, is never on time, not even to greet the Regent of Carpathia (Olivier). Just as the strap of Marilyn's dress broke at a press conference shortly before the film was made (Judith Crist supplied the safety pin), Elsie's strap breaks in the presence of the Grand Duke.

Like Cherie, Elsie is rather stupid. Her major preoccupation in the first scenes of the film is with whether she has anything appropriate to wear. She endlessly confuses the proper form of address for a Grand Duke and at one point calls him "Your Imperiousness." The joke has become quite stale midway through the film. She lacks confidence in herself, as do most of Marilyn's screen characters. "Why should he want *me*?" she asks. Elsie is, in fact, once again the sexy chorus girl. She stamps out of the Regent's palace when she finds that only two places have been set for supper because she is innocent at heart. Like Marilyn, she has another, less felicitous, name, "Elsa Stolzenburg."

What adds some measure of grace to so outworn and banal a plot is the innocence Marilyn imparts to the character of Elsie Marina. She is outraged by the Regent's arbitrary arrest of a man without charges. Her patriotism, however, is cloying. She becomes upset when Olivier criticizes the United States Government . Nonetheless, what is important to her is a concern for justice, and she effects a balance of power between the Regent and his son by the end of the film. Elsie is sincere in her personal belief that the general elections would benefit Carpathia, although the premise that America is concerned about the absence of democracy or free elections is a bit of dated propaganda.

Elsie also teaches the Grand Duke the capacity to feel and to make room in his life for "real love." But she is utterly child-like and not a person to take seriously. The Regent describes her as having

LET'S MAKE LOVE (1960). With Yves Montand

the "mind of a backward child" and later as "an unruly child." And Elsie is made to say, in weak acknowledgment, "Well, I've never grown up, I admit, and I've never wanted to, either." The Regent's young son can only say on behalf of Marilyn Monroe's fans, "You make childhood enchanting."

In the first half of the film, the Duke seeks to seduce Elsie, but when she falls in love with him, he fails to take her seriously. Elsie now attempts to seduce the Grand Duke. Marilyn's acting is self-conscious and forced. She evidently detested what she was doing, as was further indicated by the great bitterness on the set between her and Olivier. Miraculously and unconvincingly, the Regent is transformed into a loving man through contact with Elsie, from whom he must part because she is a showgirl. References to a Duke of Windsor character indicate that such a marriage, in flagrant rebellion against barriers of class, can lead only to unhappiness.

At the end Elsie is alone. Monroe's final exit is the one redeeming moment in a dreary film. She conveys enormous sweetness, innocence and a touching simplicity as she packs the gift brooches, clutching under her arm, the photographs of the royal family. The focus is on her back, but for once the point is not to accentuate her behind. The sexy walk made famous in *Niagara* has been dropped and her back to the camera, slightly bowed in grief, supports the atmosphere she created, imparting the depth of feeling with which she accepts her fate, even while savoring memories of her brief moments with the Grand Duke. In an otherwise silly film, Marilyn's vulnerability and sweetness alone make the viewing tolerable.

Some Like It Hot (1959) followed. The comedy centers entirely on the female impersonations of Jack Lemmon and Tony Curtis, running from gangsters after witnessing an underworld crime. They join an all-girl band where they meet its singer, Sugar Kane (Marilyn). True to the stereotyped roles Marilyn was always given, she is again in quest of a millionaire. Like the real Marilyn, she is too fond of her alcohol. Despite director Billy Wilder's injunction, Marilyn refused to lose weight for the part, commenting, "Don't you want your audience to be able to distinguish me from Tony and Jack? Besides, my husband likes me plump." By now Marilyn simply took for granted the superficiality of both her films and her roles in them. Regressing, she sometimes continued to think in old terms. She became very upset because the film was not in color.

LET'S MAKE LOVE (1960). As Amanda

and she was more difficult on the set than ever before. For one scene alone, she demanded fifty-nine takes. When Tony Curtis was asked about their famous love scene on the yacht, he replied bitterly that kissing Marilyn was like "kissing Hitler," so far had her relations deteriorated with the other members of the cast.

Like the gold-diggers in *How To Marry A Millionaire,* Marilyn plays a girl who longs for a rich husband, but who ultimately settles for a poor one whom she loves. Racing to the yacht supposedly belonging to Curtis, she murmurs, "It's the thought that counts." She is the familiar screen Marilyn with her crassness redeemed by openness: "It's not how long it takes," she says, "it's who's taking you." As Elsie Marina forever mixed up the title of the Grand Duke, so Sugar Kane calls the yacht a "cruiser" or a "destroyer." She labels trophies "silverware," and asks, with wonderment, "how did they get those big fish in those little jars?"

When Curtis tries to conceal his plan to seduce her by faking impotence, she replies with that sympathy which was her trademark: "That makes me feel just awful... is it that hopeless? Have you ever tried American girls?" Curtis tricks Sugar into seducing *him* by playing up to her naïveté and good heart, a task that does not prove difficult.

True to her film form, for this, her big scene, Marilyn wears a dress cut down to a V in back. Her breasts seem totally visible. She is a wide-eyed blonde who used to "sell kisses for the milk fund," and she works hard to attract Curtis because he has an even million.

Both Curtis and Lemmon are assumed by Sugar to be female members of the band. Consequently, each time she leaves Curtis, she confides all to him as "Josephine." She knocks at "Josephine's" door upon leaving the yacht, and her description of her time with him sums up her brainlessness. "It was," she gushes, "suicidally beautiful."

The film ends with a classic chase. The humor, as it has throughout the film, centers on Curtis and Lemmon. Monroe has been "window dressing" all along. Her role reduces itself to one tone and one thought. Curtis calls to break off their romance because he must flee, and Sugar reports the content of a dream she just had: "You were the captain and I was the crew." When she learns that she is to be left behind, she reaches for the bourbon bottle which she will return "when it's empty."

There is in Sugar Kane the same pathetic quality that Cherie evoked in *Bus Stop* when she attempted to emulate Hildegarde the chanteuse. It is the same hapless defeat suffered by Elsie Marina when she walks off alone at the end of *Showgirl*, despite the Regent's promise that they can be together in eighteen months. Sugar's final number declares in clichéd bathos: "I'm through with love/I'll never fall again." We are not permitted to forget, however, that it is only her body that is desirable. Wilder dresses her in a black dress which is virtually a negligee, sheer at the breasts and with spangles below.

The contrived "turn" at the end of the film has Sugar choose Curtis despite the fact that he's poor. "I told you," she informs us all, "I'm not very bright." The true owner of the yacht, Joe E. Brown, insists upon maintaining his engagement to Lemmon even upon discovering he is a man in woman's dress because "nobody's perfect." Marilyn becomes no more than a supporting member of the cast, for her presence has been only peripheral to the action of the film, despite the semblance of star billing.

Marilyn's next-to-last film, *Let's Make Love* (1960), is undoubtedly one of her worst. The film was a vehicle for Yves Montand who plays, this time, a billionaire. He falls in love with (whom else?) the showgirl Marilyn. And again the man's identity is disguised, this time to allow him certainty that she loves him for himself rather than for his money. Clement (Montand)

LET'S MAKE LOVE (1960). With Frankie Vaughan

learns of an Off-Broadway show which mocks his playboy billionaire life. He decides to try out for the part of himself, pretending to be an inexperienced actor. Marilyn tries to help and comfort him in his awkwardness as a performer, never knowing he is the real Clement auditioning to play himself.

Marilyn is again the hapless uneducated singer. She tries to better herself by attending high school at night, as Marilyn herself enrolled at UCLA for extension courses. There is one minor variation to her screen persona in *Let's Make Love*. She doesn't care at all about riches and is willing to fall in love with a poor man.

Marilyn looks very ill in this film, pasted together and not quite real. Her lips turn up artificially at the corners, her eyes crinkle unnaturally and her face is thin and unsensuous. She is visibly tired. Her childish, whispery voice now sounds stupid and lacking in range, as do her facial expressions. Even at the climactic moment when she realizes that Montand is not an inexperienced, hungry actor, but the billionaire Jean-Marc Clement, she cannot summon a deeper emotion than petulance. When she collapses in a faint at the news, it appears like the collapse of the woman behind the actress.

As usual, the role itself does not provide her with the opportunity to feel anything beyond the superficial. She is restricted to ordinary curiosity or easy sympathy. She is again vapid, forever knitting a big white amorphous mass of wool without any idea of what it is to be. "It keeps my hands busy," she says feebly. Clement tells her his name is, absurdly, "Alexander Dumas." She knows she's heard the name somewhere and nods sagely, declaring, "It's a small world." Like all the women Monroe was condemned to play, she is content to remain sheltered in a small, limited world uninvaded by history, sociology, current affairs, literature or any experiences beyond those on the set of the vulgar off-Broadway show in which she is featured.

Like the usual Monroe character, Amanda is sweet to Clement when he tells appalling jokes or is accused of stealing his only good one. But sweetness cannot carry this endless film, nor can Marilyn's song, "My Heart Belongs To Daddy," recalling the "Da-Da-Daddy" number of *Ladies of the Chorus*. The song suggests as well her calling Dougherty "daddy" and Arthur Miller "papa." The script's occasional impersonations of the real Monroe are painful and embarrassing, as when she gives Montand a demonstration of the Stanislavski method: "Imagine you can have anything you want—a limousine." At that moment Clement's

THE MISFITS (1961). As Roslyn

limousine turns the corner waiting for him. The joke, again, is on her.

When he first sees Marilyn, Montand's manager, Wilfrid Hyde-White, delightedly rubs his hands and says cynically, "There'll be children." Marilyn is once again "the body," but now pitiful, anachronistic and tired. She is sympathetic to us not as the screen character who never seems like a real person, but as the woman who through her screen character must plead, "I can't stand it when anyone makes fun of me."

All the wit belongs to Montand as he gradually assumes before her eyes his real identity as Clement. She makes a fool of herself trying to drag him off to a psychiatrist because she thinks he has delusions. He goes to his penthouse office. She accompanies him, unaware that it is his own office staff greeting them, and she fears for his sanity. When his identity dawns on her, her mouth opens, her head cocks to one side, her eyes are wide, and she looks crushed. Like the irrational and childish woman she has always played, she can only faint and then run. She slides awkwardly in her high hells on the polished floors and nearly crashes head-first into the elevator.

Clement loves her because she was willing to take jobs to support them both, because money is nothing to her and because she is lovely. Despite her anger at having been completely humiliated and rendered a fool, when he traps her in his private elevator, she dreamily rests her head on his shoulder, content to let the burdens of life fall from her as she literally collapses in his arms.

The showgirl whose father was a Reverend finds happiness with a billionaire and Hollywood whispers to its female audience, it can happen to you if you are sweet, sexy and brainless, or at least affect to be. Montand croons "Let's Make Love." Marilyn removes the jacket of her dress, simpering, "It's warm in here." Her last line is "Will they be surprised in night school!" Her schooling is presented as no more than a pretense at learning so she can grasp "what people are referring to." Having caught her man, her studies are ended and her mind need no longer expand. She lives through her body alone, and her brain may just as well contract and atrophy.

The Misfits (1961), Marilyn Monroe's last film, is generally thought to be Arthur Miller's affectionate biography of his wife. The script was written during happier times, before the hostile days of shooting in Nevada. The first description of Roslyn-Marilyn in the screenplay is of a "golden girl," beautiful but vulnerable with "a

THE MISFITS (1961). With Thelma Ritter and Clark Gable

part of her . . . totally alone, like a little child in a new school, mystified as to how it got here and passionately looking for a friendly face."

Like Marilyn, Roslyn had an unhappy childhood and a mother who abandoned her. "How," she asks, "do you *have* somebody who disappears all the time?" Like Marilyn as well, she never finished high school, although Gay Langland (Clark Gable), a cowboy and one of the only "real men" remaining, doesn't mind because he fears and dislikes educated women: "They're always wantin' to know what you're *thinkin'*."

Gay calls Roslyn "the saddest girl I ever met," as Miller felt about his vulnerable wife. "You been fooled an awful lot, haven't you?" he asks her. The script reads: "With a certain shame that is without self-pity, she whispers: Yes!" Miller depicts her as a woman who can say "I don't know where I belong... a woman whose life has forbidden her to forsake her loneliness."

Marilyn Monroe made this film fully intending to play not the sexy dumb blonde of industry promotion, but how she felt about herself. Gone was all pretense. She was much heavier than she had been in earlier films, and John Huston left in the final cut a shot of a particularly plump Marilyn emerging from the sea in a bikini.

During the shooting of the horse lassoing sequence near the end of the film, Marilyn noticed that one of the bound horses was bleeding from a cut in the chest. Just as Roslyn would have, she insisted to John Huston that the horse be spared any further shooting. Marilyn also opposed the addition of a new scene which implied that she was an ex-lover of Guido (Eli Wallach), the former air-force pilot and friend of Gay Langland. She considered it out of character. The woman she was playing was a free spirit, but not one indiscriminate with her feelings. Clark Gable, the only star with the right of script approval, vetoed the scene. The measure of male domination was that even with a script written for her personally by her husband, Gable and not she was empowered to exercise a veto on script changes.

The film's definition of freedom is self-employment, not working for wages or a boss. This expressed as well Marilyn's own desire to escape the studios. More than any film of her career, she plays herself as she really was. Her kindness is expressed toward animals, the rabbits who eat Gay's lettuce patch, Gay's dog, and finally the mustangs the men track to sell as dog food. She is governed by sympathy for people hurt and exposed like Perce Howland (Montgomery Clift), who is injured twice in the rodeo, and who has been displaced from his mother and his inheritance by an interloper.

Roslyn evidences undiluted compassion, even for the husband she is about to divorce: "I'm not blaming you ... I just don't believe in the whole thing any more." She cannot bring herself to acknowledge that her husband resorted to physical violence against her and declares that she hates to fight with anyone. To Guido's chagrin, she is more sympathetic toward his dead wife than toward him. When Guido tells her that he and his wife never danced together, Roslyn asks him why he didn't teach her to be graceful. He argues that grace is something that can't be learned, but she continues, "How do you know? I mean, how do you *know?*"

The Misfits was the most expensive black-and-white film ever made up to that time. Huston said

THE MISFITS (1961). With Montgomery Clift

on its completion that Marilyn Monroe was "all sensitivity in the film—and quite unformed." She is sensitive because she is so intimately herself; she is unformed because, like the real-life Marilyn, Roslyn is a mixture of a perceptive human being and a woman strangely unaware that her body stirs and attracts people, causing situations in which only trouble can ensue, as in the paddle-ball sequence when she is molested by an aroused onlooker.

But she is also the Hollywood Marilyn. Her voice is whispery. As she looks flirtatiously at Gable, she is luminous, tremulous and her expression is mobile. As an old dancehall teacher, she enjoys showing off her figure. She dances off by herself under the trees like a free spirit of nature, ending by clasping a tree trunk. Yet she is also a person fully in the life process at these best moments when she allows her spirit to suffuse a scene, and when Huston and Miller cease focusing on her rump.

Roslyn is also the woman who is self-sacrificing and all-giving, as Hollywood had long conditioned women to believe they must be. She tells Gay, "I want you to do what you feel like," and it is revealingly this which makes him feel she is "someone who has respect for a man." She cleans and fixes up the house Guido abandoned when his wife died; inspired by his love for her, Gay helps. To women who ask nothing for themselves, men like Huston and Miller allow the tribute that they have "the gift of life."

As Roslyn, Marilyn carries the film. The other characters are male stereotypes, but she is a person without guile, role-playing, or hypocrisy. Her feelings are close to the surface, and her vulnerability inspires decency. Perce, recognizing this, warns her not to "let them grind you up." She allies herself with all living things, refusing protection for herself if they are threatened. As she becomes disillusioned with the men around her, Roslyn surmises, "Maybe all there is is the next thing that happens." By not demanding anything for herself, she leaves herself open to the feelings of others and to the savouring of each life experience. She longs only to be certain of a man who is "kind."

Gay's violence toward the horses loosens her hold on reality, which is as precarious as was Marilyn's own. She tries physically to prevent Gay from trapping the horses. When the mare and colt are run down, felled and tied up, Roslyn runs off screaming, calling the three men killers and liars: "Why don't you kill yourselves . . . you're three dead men." Aided by her training in the Stanislavsky method, Marilyn makes the

THE MISFITS (1961). With Clark Gable

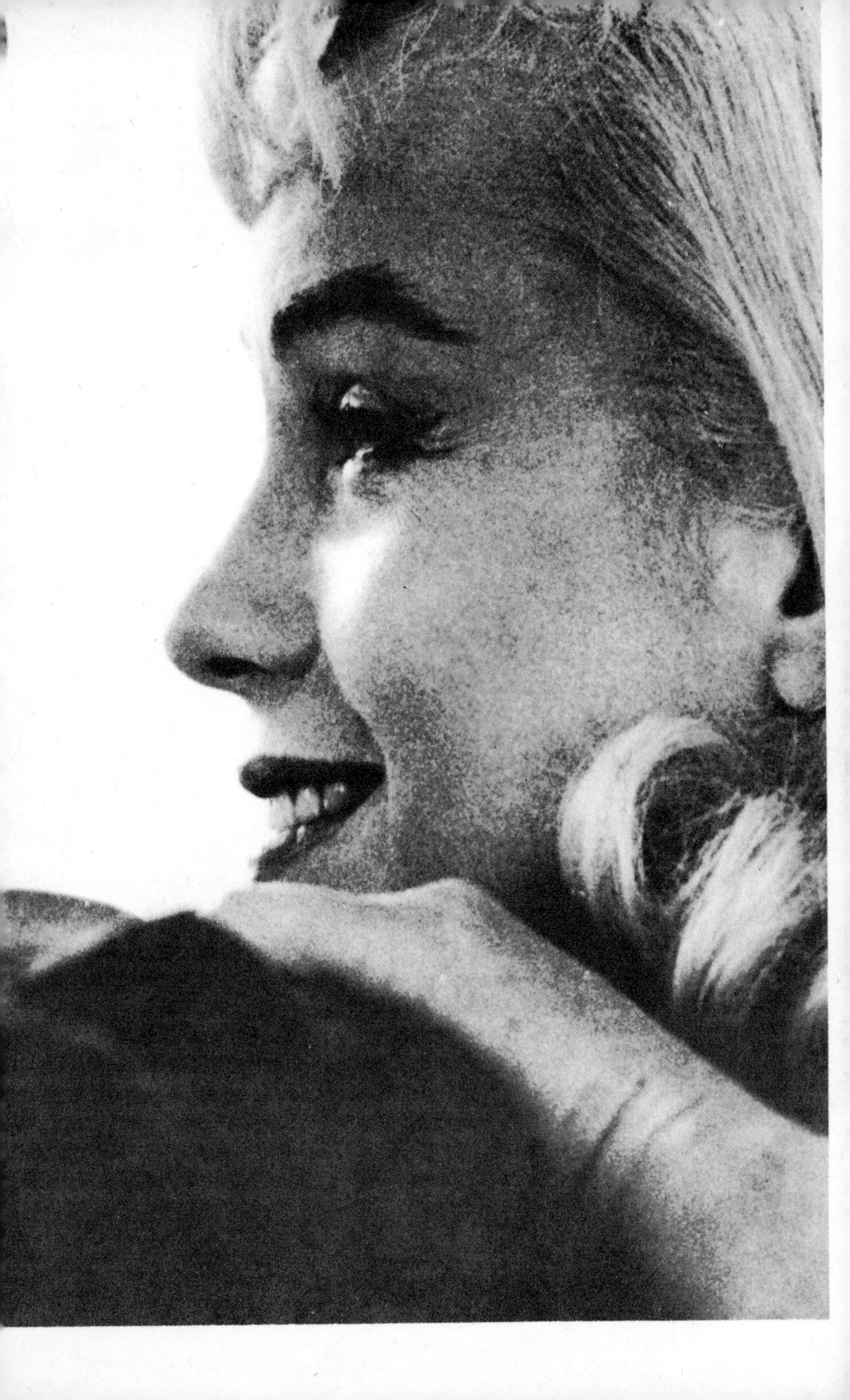

THE MISFITS (1961). With Clark Gable

THE MISFITS (1961). With Clark Gable, heading for the "star" that will take them "right home"

moment direct, real, deeply felt and potent. It is the dramatic climax of a film with a very thin narrative line, and it permits the final resolution in which the horses are freed and Roslyn consequently reconciled with Gay.

They head for "that big star straight on" that will take them "right home." It is the first time that Marilyn is truly at the center of one of her films; it is from her character that the capacity for justice expressed by Gay springs.

Marilyn Monroe did not live to become the serious actress of her avowed aspirations. All that is genuine which remains for us to remember are her characterizations of Roslyn and Cherie, into which so many strands of her real personality are interwoven. It is as Roslyn, especially, that the sympathy and respect for the woman Marilyn Monroe are commanded. Even so, the sexual display which she still would not relinquish establishes simultaneously why neither she nor the people for whom she worked could allow her to grow and develop as she needed and craved. Roslyn begins to transcend, but falls short. Through her can be felt the homage Marilyn Monroe deserves for her extraordinary struggle.

But the fact that it was only in her last completed film that this occurs indicates how thorough and irretrievable was the damage done to her. In all of her films she is made to mock herself, not only through caricature, but even in ridicule of her own intellectual and emotional aspirations. Hollywood finally accomplished its self-fulfilling prophecy. It made her not only on the screen, but also in life her own executioner.

CHAPTER VI

NOTES ON THE DEATH OF MARILYN MONROE

It might be kind of a relief to be finished. It's sort of like I don't know what kind of a yard dash you're running, but then you're at the finish line and you sort of sigh—you've made it! But you never have—you have to start all over again.

Marilyn Monroe.

Marilyn Monroe saw her life as a race and an interminable struggle to achieve an ever-elusive goal. At the age of thirty-six she was not yet able to accept or achieve the mature persona of Marilyn Monroe, an identity which was the unripened fruit of long years of very hard work as an actress. Although the directors with whom she worked were often exasperated by her lateness and illnesses, none would deny that she was one of the most indefatigable workers they had known. Yet she could never feel that she had achieved the obliteration of the needy foster child Norma Jean nor accomplish the final struggle to determine once and for all that she had become the woman of her own creation.

Her deepest feelings remained those of Norma Jean. By seeking to obliterate these feelings as a way of becoming confident and accomplished, she was destroying herself. Ironically, this suppression placed her more firmly in the injurious sway of the past, until only massive doses of narcotizing drugs could allay the unresolved pain. As her therapy proved inadequate and her profession put her in the destructive hands of Hollywood, her fate was ultimately sealed. Only great courage kept her going as long as she did.

Many have speculated on the causes of her suicide in 1962. Clare Boothe Luce wrote in *Life* that Marilyn killed herself so that she would not have to face old age and the waning of her beauty: "Surely she realized that the mob worship of her for her pure sexuality could not last more than a few years longer. Breasts, belly, bottom must one day sag. She was thirty-six, and her mirror had begun to warn her." But, belying Luce, at the end Marilyn spoke of becoming a character actress. Right before her death, she said, "I feel I'm just getting started; I want to do comedy, tragedy, interspersed. . . ." She did not see herself as the sex symbol Mrs. Luce insists solely defined her. She would no doubt have felt relief no longer to be forced into that role.

Some have felt that she sought help in the wrong places, from the very men who were attracted to her precisely because of her image Such men were hardly likely to encourage her in the difficult struggle to relinquish the image of Marilyn Monroe for a more precarious existence as an actress who would have to survive on her ability rather than on her looks. Diana Trilling has remarked presciently on the boon to Marilyn's consciousness women friends could have made in her life. "We," says Mrs. Trilling, "were the friends of whom she knew nothing."

Many of Marilyn's remarks after 1960 indicate her feeling that an early death was inevitable and the struggle too difficult to sustain. It is as if she were trying to convince herself to endure. At the time of *The Misfits* and the dissolution of her marriage to Miller, she stated, "I want to survive," a comment possible only from a person with serious doubts about the value of continuing. Immediately before her death, she said, "As far as I'm concerned there's a future and I can't wait to get to it," as if she felt some need to convince the world that she was not already dead, and had to prove that she had not yet given up on life.

Toward the end a cruel streak in the personality of Marilyn Monroe became increasingly apparent. She was rude to technicians on the sets of *The Prince And The Showgirl*, *Some Like It Hot*, and *Let's Make Love*. She quarreled with cameramen and would then apologize. On the set of *Some Like It Hot*, she used a four-letter word when an assistant director knocked on her dressing-room door to call her to work. And during the shooting of *Bus Stop* when Don Murray was required to rip the train off her dress, she snatched it and slashed it across his face, cutting him in several places. She would not apologize.

Similar incidents happened in her personal life as well. When she met her former brother-in-law, Tom Dougherty, in 1961 and he invited her to visit his family, she retorted, "How much is it going to cost me?" When her father tried to contact her from a hospital, she gave him the same message he had once given her: "If he has anything specific to tell me, he can contact my lawyer. Would you like his number?"

The pressures of being Marilyn Monroe had gotten to her, calling forth the hostility at a world that had done her wrong, resentments which had always lain hidden beneath her natural sweetness. The realization that all her success had brought her only loneliness and pain, the very pain with which she had begun, proved to be too much. In another of his fits of pique, Arthur Miller dedicated the screenplay of *The Misfits* to "Clark

SOMETHING'S GOT TO GIVE (1962. uncompleted). With Wally Cox

SOMETHING'S GOT TO GIVE (1962, uncompleted)

Gable, who did not know how to hate," a psychologically absurd remark laden with implications against Marilyn. On the contrary, she might have lived had she learned to hate much earlier and found the courage to refuse to play the deadly game Hollywood had set up for her. She might have demanded roles in which she would have been sexually attractive to no one. And she might have survived better had Norma Jean been truly allowed to express herself.

In 1961 Marilyn Monroe was voluntarily committed to the Payne Whitney Clinic in New York, a hospital for mental patients. She signed herself in as "Faye Miller," still wishing to keep the woman Marilyn Monroe separate from the real self struggling to be heard. She was placed on the floor reserved for the most highly disturbed patients and kept under twenty-four-hour surveillance to prevent her from harming herself after she had broken the glass door of her bathroom with her shoes and fists.

Miserable and unable to come to terms with this portion of herself, she arranged to be transferred to the Neurological Institute of Columbia-Presbyterian Medical Center four days later. She remained there for twenty-three days. Around this time there was a suicide attempt from an open window, one of many such attempts in her life. Two occurred before she was nineteen, one by pills and one by gas. If her death would be called an "accident" by some, it was certainly not unprecedented.

On August 5, 1962, the last night of her life, Marilyn Monroe called her psychiatrist for help. He suggested, incredibly, that she go out for an automobile ride, like the compulsive Maria Wyeth in Joan Didion's novel, *Play It As It Lays*, who drove the Los Angeles freeways in desperation. Such advice only points up the inability of psychoanalysis to help Marilyn, despite her long years of treatment. Its methods were too weak to reconcile the divided halves of the personality of Marilyn Monroe, the split between feeling and consciousness.

She died in a sparsely furnished bedroom, more bare and unlived-in than the dreariest hotel room. Although she had taken a very large overdose of Nembutal, the actual circumstances of her death remain a mystery. The chemical analysis of her autopsy revealed not only the expected Nembutal and chloral hydrate or "knock-out drops" that she had been taking, but the presence of burns in her mouth and digestive tract and a fast-acting poison in her stomach. This finding points, without question, to suicide since there was no one else in her house that night other than herself and a housekeeper. When she was found, her door was locked from the inside.

Doctors testified that she "had suffered from psychiatric disturbance for a long time. She experienced severe fears and frequent depressions—mood changes were abrupt and unpredictable." They ruled that she was "psychologically" dependent on drugs. Indeed she had reached a point of malfunction where she was unable to work. She had appeared on the set of *Something's Got To Give* only twelve times in thirty-two days of shooting and had been fired.

The remaining footage of that film reveals a Marilyn in a state of hysteria, even in the takes of her costume tests. Her eyes glitter nervously, her laughter seems uncontrollable, she flaunts herself. The costume tests reveal as well an older Marilyn, still beautiful, still possessing an exquisite figure, but with lines appearing around her mouth and eyes. It was a Marilyn who could not readily suppress pre-conscious, vital urgings. Although her screen character could always gain roots from having become involved with a man stronger than herself, the real Marilyn had found no man capable of helping ease the burden of her tortured self. Thrown back upon her own resources, her psyche collapsed in panic and defeat.

The police, strangely, refused to name the poison found in Marilyn Monroe. Even more astounding was their impounding of the telephone company's taped record of her outgoing calls on the night of her death. This indicated a call Marilyn made to someone whose help she craved, but whose high public position could not survive the scandal of being linked with her. She died with the telephone in her hand.

SOMETHING'S GOT TO GIVE (1962, uncompleted)

BIBLIOGRAPHY

Anderson, Lilla. "The Girl You Know As Marilyn," *Photoplay*, January, 1955.

Anonymous. *Violations of the Child Marilyn Monroe*. New York, Bridgehead Books, 1962.

Barbour, William. "Why Joe Let Her Go," *Modern Screen*, January, 1955.

Bessie, Alvah. *The Symbol*. New York, Random House, 1966.

Bolstad, Helen. "Marilyn In The House," *Photoplay*, September, 1955.

Carpozi, Jr; George. *Marilyn Monroe-Her Own Story*. New York, Belmont Books, 1961.

Conway, Michael, and Ricci, Mark. *The Films Of Marilyn Monroe*. Secaucus, New Jersey, The Citadel Press, 1972.

Corbin, Julia. "Will She Break Joe's Heart Again?", *Photoplay*, April, 1961.

Corwin, Jane. "Orphan In Ermine," *Photoplay*, March, 1954.

Dean, Bob. "Marilyn's Secret Marriage Plans," *Photoplay*, May, 1961.

De Blaseo, Ed. "We Find Her Father and Sister," *Photoplay*, December, 1962

Dinter, Charlotte. "What She Couldn't Tell The Doctor." *Photoplay*, October, 1959.

Donnelly, Tom. "Marilyn Focuses My Attention," *New York World Telegram & Sun*, June 11; 1957.

Dougherty, James. "Marilyn Monroe Was My Wife," *Photoplay*, March, 1953.

Durán, Manuel. *Vida Y Muerte de un Mito*. Mexico City, Dirección General de Difusion Cultural, UNAM, 1965.

Evans, Clarice. "Why Marilyn And Joe Broke Up," *This Week Magazine*, November 28, 1954.

Ford, Eve. "Journey Into Paradise," *Photoplay*, April, 1954.

Franklin, J., and Palmer, L. *The Marilyn Monroe Story*. New York, 1953.

Giglio, Tommaso, *Marilyn Monroe*. Parma, Guanda, 1956.

Goode, James. *The Story Of The Misfits*. New York, Bobbs Merrill, 1963.

Graham, Sheila. "Why Gentlemen Prefer Blondes," *Photoplay*, June, 1953.

Guerney, Jr., Otis L. "Problem: How To Display Marilyn Monroe's Talents," *New York Herald Tribune*, May 19, 1954.

Guiles, Fred Lawrence. *Norma Jean: The Life of Marilyn Monroe*. New York, Bantam, 1970.

Harris, Radie. "The Empty Crib In The Nursery," *Photoplay*, December, 1958.

Hattersley, Ralph. "Marilyn Monroe: The Image And Her Photographers," *Popular Photography*, January, 1966.

Hoffman, Alice. "The Only Complete Story of Marilyn Monroe's Honeymoon," *Modern Screen*, April, 1954.

Hopper, Hedda. "Marilyn Monroe Tells The Truth to Hedda Hopper," *Photoplay*, January, 1953.
Hoyt, Edwin P. *Marilyn Monroe: The Tragic Venus*. New York, Duell, Sloan and Pearce, 1965.
Johnson, Hildegarde. "Hollywood vs. Marilyn Monroe," *Photoplay*, July, 1953.
Joyce, Alex. "Marilyn At The Crossroads," *Photoplay*, June, 1957.
Kirstein, Lincoln. "Marilyn Monroe: 1926-1962," *The Nation*, August 25, 1962.
Kutner, Nanette. "Don't Blame Yourself, Marilyn," *Photoplay*, January, 1955.
Laclos, Michel. *Marilyn Monroe*. Paris, J. Pauvert, 1962.
Levy, Alan. "A Good Long Look At Myself," *Redbook*, August, 1962.
Life. "Remember Marilyn," September 8, 1972.
Luce, Clare Boothe. "What Really Killed Marilyn," *Life*, August 7, 1964.
Lyle, Joe. "Behind The Yves Montand, Marilyn Monroe, Arthur Miller Triangle," *Photoplay*, October, 1960.
Manning, Dorothy. "The Woman And The Legend," *Photoplay*, October, 1956.
Marilyn, Screen Great Series No. 4, ed. Milburn Smith, New York: Barven Publications, Inc., 1971
Marilyn Monroe As The Girl, photographed by Sam Shaw, foreword by George Axelrod. New York, Ballantine Books, 1955.
Martin, Pete. *Will Acting Spoil Marilyn Monroe?* New York, Doubleday and Company, Inc., 1956.
Meltsir, Aljean. "Marilyn Monroe's Final Tribute," *Photoplay*, November, 1962.
Meryman, Richard. "Interview with Marilyn Monroe," *Life*, August 3, 1962.
Michaels, Evans. "What Was Marilyn Monroe Doing at 685 Third Avenue?" *Photoplay*, August, 1959.
Miller, Arthur. *The Misfits*. New York, Dell, 1961.
Miller, Arthur. *After The Fall: A Play In Two Acts*. New York, The Viking Press, 1964.
Monroe, Marilyn. "Make It For Keeps," *Photoplay*, July, 1951.
Monroe, Marilyn. "I Want Women To Like Me," *Photoplay*, November, 1952.
Monroe, Marilyn. "My Beauty Secrets," *Photoplay*, October, 1953.
Moore, Isabel. "If Marilyn Has A Little Girl," *Photoplay*, October, 1954.
Newsweek. "Taking A New Look At MM," October 16, 1972.
Parish, James Robert. *The Fox Girls*. New Rochelle, New York, Arlington House, 1971.
Pascal, John. *Marilyn Monroe–The Complete Story Of Her Life, Her Loves and Her Death*. New York, 1962.
Peabody, Marjorie. "The Woman Arthur Miller Went To When He Walked Out On Marilyn Monroe," *Photoplay*, February, 1961.
Photoplay. "He's Her Joe," July, 1952.
Photoplay. "The Private Life Of Joe and Marilyn," December, 1953.
Photoplay. "Divorce," December, 1960.
Photoplay. "Desperate," September, 1962.
Rattigan, Terence. *The Prince And The Showgirl*. New York, Signet, 1957.
Reiner, Silvain. *La Tragedie de Marilyn Monroe*. Paris, Plon, 1965.
Roman, Robert C. "Marilyn Monroe: Her Tragedy Was Allowing Herself To Be Misled Intellectually," *Films In Review*, October, 1962.
Schickel, Richard. *The Stars*. New York, The Dial Press, 1962.
Schreiber, Flora Rheta. "Remembrance of Marilyn," *Good Housekeeping*, January, 1963.
Serini, Maria Livia. *Norma Jeane Baker: Flu nota come Marilyn Monroe*. Milano, Trevi, 1961.
Skolsky, Sidney. "Marilyn Monroe's Honeymoon Whirl," *Photoplay*, May, 1954.
Skolsky, Sidney. "260,000 Minutes of Marriage," *Photoplay*, August, 1954.

Smith, Sterling, "On The Spot With Marilyn Monroe," *Photoplay*, January, 1954.
Steinem, Gloria. "The Woman Who Died Too Soon," *Ms*, August, 1972.
Strasberg, Lee. "Remarks At The Funeral," *New York Herald Tribune*, August 9, 1962.
Tracy, Jacy. "Is It A Thing—Or Is It A Fling," *Photoplay*, September, 1961.
Trilling, Diana. "The Death of Marilyn Monroe," *Claremont Essays*. New York, Harcourt, Brace and World, 1963.
Wagenknecht, Edward. "Rosemary For Remembrance," *Seven Daughters Of The Theatre*. Oklahoma City, University of Oklahoma Press, 1964.
Wagenknecht, Edward, ed. *Marilyn Monroe: A Composite View*. Philadelphia, Chilton Book Company, 1969.
Walker, Alexander. "Body and Soul: Harlow and Monroe," *The Celluloid Sacrifice*. New York, Hawthorn Books, 1966.
Watt, Douglas. "A Word Of Advice To A Poor Wandering Girl," *New York Daily News*, July 12, 1955.
Wilson, Earl. "The Things She Said To Me," *Photoplay*, May, 1956.
Zanetti, Livio. *Marilyn Monroe*. Milano, Sedit, 1955.
Zolotow, Maurice. *Marilyn Monroe*. New York, Harcourt, Brace and Company, 1960.

THE FILMS OF MARILYN MONROE

The director's name follows the release date. A (c) following the release date indicates that the film was in color. Sp indicates Screenplay and b/o indicates based/on.

1. SCUDDA HOO! SCUDDA HAY! 20th Century-Fox, 1948. (c) *F. Hugh Herbert.* Sp: F. Hugh Herbert, b/o novel by George Agnew Chamberlain. Cast: June Haver, Lon McCallister. Marilyn as a friend of June Haver winds up on the cutting-room floor.

2. DANGEROUS YEARS. 20th Century-Fox, 1948. *Arthur Pierson.* Sp: Arnold Belgard, b/o story by Belgard. Cast: William Halop, Ann E. Todd, Jerome Cowan. Marilyn in a bit part as a waitress in a teenage hangout.

3. LADIES OF THE CHORUS. Columbia, 1948. *Phil Karlson.* Sp: Harry Sauber and Joseph Carol, b/o story by Harry Sauber. Cast: Adele Jergens, Rand Brooks. Marilyn as a burlesque queen who marries a rich admirer.

4. LOVE HAPPY. United Artists Release of Mary Pickford Presentation, 1950. *David Miller.* Sp: Frank Tashlin and Mac Benoff, b/o story by Harpo Marx. Cast: Harpo, Chico, and Groucho Marx, Ilona Massey, Vera-Ellen. Marilyn in a walk-on as a sexy would-be client of detective Groucho.

5. A TICKET TO TOMAHAWK. 20th Century-Fox, 1950. (c) *Richard Sale.* Sp: Mary Loos and Richard Sale. Cast: Dan Dailey, Anne Baxter, Rory Calhoun, Walter Brennan. Marilyn as one of a troupe of showgirls.

6. THE ASPHALT JUNGLE. Metro-Goldwyn-Mayer, 1950. *John Huston.* Sp: Ben Maddow and John Huston, b/o novel by W. R. Burnett. Cast: Sterling Hayden, Louis Calhern, Jean Hagen, Sam Jaffe, James Whitmore. Marilyn is the mistress ("niece") who betrays crooked lawyer Calhern.

7. ALL ABOUT EVE. 20th Century-Fox, 1950. *Joseph L. Mankiewicz.* Sp: Joseph L. Mankiewicz, b/o story by Mary Orr. Cast: Bette Davis, Anne Baxter, George Sanders, Celeste Holm, Gary Merrill. Marilyn as dumb blonde, Miss Caswell, graduate of "the Copacabana School of Dramatic Arts."

8. THE FIREBALL. 20th Century-Fox Release of a Thor Production, 1950. *Tay Garnett.* Sp: Tay Garnett and Horace McCoy. Cast: Mickey Rooney, Pat O'Brien, Beverly Tyler. One of the many women interested in roller-skater Rooney is Marilyn.

9. RIGHT CROSS. Metro-Goldwyn-Mayer, 1950. *John Sturges.* Sp: Charles Schnee. Cast: June Allyson, Dick Powell, Ricardo Montalban, Lionel Barrymore. Marilyn in a bit role as a distraction for Powell, who is really in love with Allyson.

10. HOMETOWN STORY. Metro-Goldwyn-Mayer, 1951. *Arthur Pierson.* Sp: Arthur Pierson. Cast: Jeffrey Lynn, Donald Crisp, Marjorie Reynolds, Alan Hale, Jr. Marilyn as a secretary in a newspaper office.

11. AS YOUNG AS YOU FEEL. 20th Century-Fox, 1951. *Harmon Jones.* Sp: Lamar Trotti, b/o story by Paddy Chayefsky. Cast: Monty Woolley, Thelma Ritter, David Wayne, Jean Peters. Marilyn again as a secretary.

12. LOVE NEST. 20th Century-Fox, 1951. *Joseph Newman.* Sp: I. A. L. Diamond, b/o novel by Scott Corbett. Cast: June Haver, William Lundigan, Frank Fay, Jack Paar. Marilyn as a former WAC who inspires the jealousy of Lundigan's wife, Haver.

13. LET'S MAKE IT LEGAL. 20th Century-Fox, 1951. *Richard Sale.* Sp: F. Hugh Herbert and I. A. L. Diamond, b/o story by Mortimer Braus. Cast: Claudette Colbert, Macdonald Carey, Zachary Scott. Marilyn as an on-the-rebound interest for Carey, still in love with wife Colbert.

14. CLASH BY NIGHT. RKO Radio Release of a Jerry Wald-Norman Krasna Production, 1952. *Fritz Lang.* Sp: Alfred Hayes, b/o play by Clifford Odets. Cast: Barbara Stanwyck, Paul Douglas, Robert Ryan. Marilyn is the fiancée of Stanwyck's younger brother.

15. WE'RE NOT MARRIED. 20th Century-Fox, 1952. *Edmund Goulding.* Sp: Nunnally Johnson, b/o story by Gina Kaus and Jay Dratler. Cast: Ginger Rogers, Fred Allen, Victor Moore, David Wayne, Eve Arden, Paul Douglas, Eddie Bracken, Mitzi Gaynor, Louis Calhern, Zsa Zsa Gabor. Marilyn as "Mrs. Mississippi" who learns that she and husband Wayne are not legally married.

16. DON'T BOTHER TO KNOCK. 20th Century-Fox, 1952. *Roy Baker.* Sp: Daniel Taradash, b/o novel by Charlotte Armstrong. Cast: Richard Widmark, Anne Bancroft, Donna Corcoran. Marilyn as a psychotic baby-sitter.

17. MONKEY BUSINESS. 20th Century-Fox, 1952. *Howard Hawks*. Sp: Ben Hecht, Charles Lederer, and I. A. L. Diamond, b/o story by Harry Segall. Cast: Cary Grant, Ginger Rogers, Charles Coburn. Marilyn as another dumb blonde secretary.

18. O. HENRY'S FULL HOUSE. 20th Century-Fox, 1952. The story in which Marilyn Monroe appears directed by *Henry Koster*. Sp: Lamar Trotti, b/o "The Cop and the Anthem" by O.Henry. Cast: Charles Laughton, David Wayne. Marilyn in a walk-on as a streetwalker accosted by Laughton.

19. NIAGARA. 20th Century-Fox, 1953. (c) *Henry Hathaway*. Sp: Charles Brackett, Walker Reisch, and Richard Breen. Cast: Joseph Cotten, Jean Peters, Casey Adams. Marilyn as a faithless wife finally murdered by her husband.

20. GENTLEMEN PREFER BLONDES. 20th Century-Fox, 1953. (c) *Howard Hawks*. Sp: Charles Lederer, b/o musical by Joseph Fields and Anita Loos. Cast: Jane Russell, Charles Coburn, Elliott Reid, Tommy Noonan. Marilyn as gold-digger Loreli Lee.

21. HOW TO MARRY A MILLIONAIRE. 20th Century-Fox, 1953. (c) *Jean Negulesco*. Sp: Nunnally Johnson, b/o plays by Zoe Akins and Dale Eunson and Katherine Albert. Cast: Betty Grable, Lauren Bacall, William Powell, David Wayne, Rory Calhoun, Cameron Mitchell. Marilyn as near-sighted Pola whose "millionaire" turns out to be a fugitive from justice.

22. RIVER OF NO RETURN. 20th Century-Fox, 1954. (c) *Otto Preminger*. Sp: Frank Fenton, b/o story by Louis Lantz. Cast: Robert Mitchum, Rory Calhoun, Tommy Rettig. Marilyn as saloon singer Kay fleeing the Indians with farmer Mitchum.

23. THERE'S NO BUSINESS LIKE SHOW BUSINESS. 20th Century-Fox, 1954. (c) *Walter Lang*. Sp: Phoebe and Henry Ephron, b/o story by Lamar Trotti. Cast: Ethel Merman, Donald O'Connor, Dan Dailey, Johnnie Ray, Mitzi Gaynor. Marilyn as sexy nightclub singer Vicky pursued by O'Connor.

24. THE SEVEN YEAR ITCH. 20th Century-Fox, 1955. (c) *Billy Wilder*. Sp: Billy Wilder and George Axelrod, b/o play by George Axelrod. Cast: Tom Ewell, Evelyn Keyes, Sonny Tufts. Marilyn, as "The Girl" upstairs, tempts summer bachelor Ewell.

25. BUS STOP. 20th Century-Fox, 1956. (c) *Joshua Logan*. Sp: George Axelrod, b/o play by William Inge. Cast: Don Murray, Arthur O'Connell, Betty Field, Eileen Heckart. Marilyn as "chantoose" Cherie pursued by brash cowboy Murray.

26. THE PRINCE AND THE SHOWGIRL. A Warner Brothers Presentation of a Film by Marilyn Monroe Productions, Inc. and L.O.P. Ltd., 1957. (c) *Laurence Olivier*. Sp: Terence Rattigan, b/o play by Terence Rattigan. Cast: Laurence Olivier, Sybil Thorndike. Marilyn as showgirl who has affair with the Grand Duke of Carpathia.

27. SOME LIKE IT HOT. United Artists Release of Mirisch Company Presentation of an Ashton Picture, 1959. *Billy Wilder*. Sp: Billy Wilder and I. A. L. Diamond, b/o suggestion from a story by Robert Thoeren and M. Logan. Cast: Tony Curtis, Jack Lemmon, George Raft, Pat O'Brien, Joe E. Brown. Marilyn as Sugar Kane, singer with an all-girl band and in love with female impersonator Curtis.

28. LET'S MAKE LOVE. 20th Century-Fox, 1960. (c) *George Cukor*. Sp: Norman Krasna. Cast: Yves Montand, Tony Randall, Frankie Vaughan, Wilfrid Hyde-White. Marilyn as Amanda who falls for billionaire Montand.

29. THE MISFITS. United Artists Release of A Seven Arts Productions Presentation of a John Huston Production, 1961. *John Huston*. Sp: Arthur Miller. Cast: Clark Gable, Montgomery Clift, Thelma Ritter, Eli Wallach. Marilyn is Roslyn, a sweet-natured divorcee finding peace with cowboy Gable.

30. SOMETHING'S GOT TO GIVE. 20th Century-Fox, 1962. *George Cukor*. Sp: Nunnally Johnson. Cast: Dean Martin, Cyd Charisse, Phil Silvers, Wally Cox. Uncompleted remake of *My Favorite Wife*, with Marilyn in Irene Dunne role.

INDEX

(Page numbers italicized indicate photographs)

M

N

O

P

R

S

T

U

V

W

Z

ABOUT THE AUTHOR

Joan Mellen is an Associate Professor at Temple University in Philadelphia where she teaches literature and film. She has published widely in such journals as *Film Quarterly, Cinema, Cineaste, Film Comment, Ms., Novel, Antioch Review, Sexual Behavior,* and *New Politics.* She is the author of the forthcoming *The Battle of Algiers* (Indiana University Press), *Women And Sex In The Cinema* (Horizon Press), and *Politics and Film* (Horizon Press). She is finishing a book for the University of California Press on social dimensions of the Japanese cinema and is at work on a novel concerning the character of the revolutionary.

ABOUT THE EDITOR

Ted Sennett has been attending and enjoying movies since the age of two. He has written about films for magazines and newspapers, and is the author of *Warner Brothers Presents,* a survey of the great Warners films of the thirties and forties. A publishing executive, he lives in New Jersey with his wife and three children.